Studien zur Mustererkennung

herausgegeben von:

Prof. Dr.-Ing. Heinrich Niemann
Prof. Dr.-Ing. Elmar Nöth

Bibliografische Information der Deutschen Nationalbibliothek

Die Deutsche Nationalbibliothek verzeichnet diese Publikation in der
Deutschen Nationalbibliografie; detaillierte bibliografische Daten sind
im Internet über http://dnb.d-nb.de abrufbar.

ISBN 978-3-8325-4583-3
ISSN 1617-0695

Logos Verlag Berlin GmbH
Comeniushof
Gubener Str. 47
10243 Berlin
Tel.: +49 030 42 85 10 90
Fax: +49 030 42 85 10 92
INTERNET: http://www.logos-verlag.de

3D Trajectory Extraction from 2D Videos for Human Activity Analysis

DISSERTATION

zur Erlangung des Grades eines Doktors

der Ingenieurwissenschaften

vorgelegt von

M.Sc. Zeyd Boukhers

geb. am 25.04.1987 in Oran

eingereicht bei der Naturwissenschaftlich-Technischen Fakultät

der Universität Siegen

Siegen 2017

Gutachter der Dissertation:

1. Prof. Dr. Marcin Grzegorzek

2. Prof. Dr. Kuniaki Uehara
(Universität Kōbe, Japan)

Tag der mündlichen Prüfung:

26. September 2017.

Acknowledgements

First and foremost, I would like to express the deepest appreciation to my supervisor *Prof. Marcin Grzegorzek* for his great assistance, effective supervision and strong encouragement from the first day of my doctoral studies. His supports have been going far beyond supervision to develop my academic knowledge, skills and abilities. Then, I wish to thank *Prof. Kuniaki Uehara* for hosting me as a visiting researcher in his laboratory and accepting to be my second supervisor. I would also like to extend my thanks to *Prof. Roland Wismüller* and *Prof. Kristof Van Laerhoven* for agreeing to serve on my examination committee.

I want to give very special thanks to *Dr. Kimiaki Shirahama* for his academic assistance and guidance, which made a crucial difference in the elaboration of this work. Moreover, I want to express my thanks to all the members and alumni of *the Research Group for Pattern Recognition* at the university of Siegen, for being professional colleagues and great friends. I am very glad to have known you and really appreciate working with you. Besides, I thank the members of the group "CS24" at Kobe university, Japan. A special thanks is owed to those who contributed in my research projects.

I am also thankful to *the German Academic Exchange Service (DAAD)* for their financial support during my doctoral studies. In particular, I would like to thank *Ms. Anke Bahrani*, whose cooperation helped me to focus on my research.

Last but not least, I can't find the words to express all my gratitude, love and and thanks to my parents and grandparents for always being with me. Finally, my greats thanks go to my brothers *Yasser* and *Mouad* and my wife *Amel*, who lived through difficult times with me.

Abstract

The present dissertation addresses the problem of extracting three dimensional (3D) trajectories of objects from two dimensional (2D) videos. The reason of this is the theory that these trajectories symbolise high-level interpretations of human activities. A 3D trajectory of an object means its sequential positions in the real world over time. To this end, a generic framework for detecting objects and extracting their trajectories is proposed, ending with applications of trajectory analysis. In this context, each step represents independent approaches dedicated to solving challenging tasks in computer vision and multimedia.

In order to analyse different human activities in image sequences, it is crucial to extract appropriate features that can express these activities. Considering 3D trajectories of objects as high-level features, the difficulty lies in their extraction from 2D videos due to the serious lack of 3D information. Starting from video frames, this dissertation introduces methods to detect objects in crowded images. In addition to the local and global characteristics, deep learning-based features are used in this process to distinguish objects from the background. The main contribution of this work is centred in the subsequent step of the framework, which is dedicated to sequentially putting objects into perspective. In simpler terms, it means obtaining the 3D coordinate of the objects detected on the image plane and then tracking them in the real world to extract their 3D trajectories. Due to the varying complexities associated with different types of videos, two different methods are proposed in this dissertation. Here, each method addresses the problem of extracting 3D trajectories of objects from videos that are taken under specific conditions, namely, surveillance and moving cameras. Lastly, two applications of trajectory-based human activity analysis in the crowd are proposed. The first application employs trajectories to detect groups of people, whereas the second application analyses the trajectories to classify the human behaviour into ordinary and suspicious.

In summary, the dissertation at hand presents several approaches, the combination of which yields the extraction of 3D trajectories of objects from 2D videos. To show the robustness of each approach and its sub-methods, detailed evaluations on public and challenging datasets are performed.

Zusammenfassung

Die vorliegende Dissertation befasst sich mit der Extrahierung von 3D Trajektorien von Objekten aus 2D Videos. Der Extrahierung der Trajektorien liegt die Theorie zugrunde, dass sie abstrakte menschliche Aktivitäten symbolisieren könnten. Die 3D Trajektorie eines Objekts steht für dessen aufeinanderfolgende Positionen in der echten Welt über einen bestimmten Zeitraum. Zu diesem Zweck wird ein allgemeines Framework zur Erkennung von Objekten und Extrahierung ihrer Trajektorien vorgestellt, welches mit der Anwendung der Trajektorie -Analyse endet. Jeder Schritt dieses Frameworks repräsentiert unabhängige Ansätze zur Lösung anspruchsvoller Aufgaben in Computervision und Multimedia. Um verschiedene menschliche Aktivitäten in Bildsequenzen zu analysieren, ist es von essentieller Bedeutung, angemessene Merkmale zu extrahieren, die diese Aktivitäten darstellen können. Unter der Annahme, dass 3D Trajektorien von Objekten Merkmale höchster Abstraktionsebene sind, liegt die Herausforderung in deren Extrahierung aus 2D Videos aufgrund des Mangels an 3D Informationen. Ausgehend von Video Frames stellt diese Dissertation Methoden vor, um Objekte in überladenen Bildern zu erkennen. Zusätzlich zu lokalen und globalen Merkmalen werden hier Deep Learning-basierte Merkmale genutzt um Objekte vom Hintergrund zu unterscheiden. Der Großteil dieser Arbeit steckt im fortführenden Schritt des Frameworks, dessen Aufgabe es ist, Objekte sequentiell in Perspektive zu setzen. Einfacher gesagt werden die 3D Koordinaten der Objekte, die auf der Bildebene erkannt wurden, gewonnen und dann in der echten Welt verfolgt, um ihre 3D Trajektorien zu erhalten. Aufgrund der unterschiedlichen Komplexität verschiedener Videotypen, werden in dieser Dissertation zwei verschiedene Methoden vorgestellt, wobei jede der beiden das Problem der Extrahierung von 3D Trajektorien aus Video, die untere besonderen Umständen aufgenommen wurden, genauer gesagt Überwachungskameras und sich bewegende Kameras, angehen. Zuletzt werden zwei Anwendungen der Analyse von menschlicher Aktivität in Menschenmengen basierend auf den Trajektorien vorgestellt. Die erste Anwendung verwendet Trajektorien, um Gruppen von Menschen zu erkennen, während die zweite Anwendung die Trajektorien analysiert, um das Verhalten der Menschen in normal und auffällig zu klassifizieren. Zusammengefasst beschreibt diese Dissertation mehrere Ansätze, die kombiniert die Extrahierung

von 3D Trajektorien aus 2D Videos analysieren. Um die Robustheit der einzelnen Methoden zu demonstrieren, wurden diese detailliert anhand öffentlicher und herausfordernder
Datensätze ausgewertet.

Contents

Chapter 1

Introduction

The fast and dramatic development of security issues in public spaces in recent years necessitates the search for an effective way to monitor objects' activities. Here, it is meant by an object, every dynamic thing whose actions are affecting and affected by its counterparts. Mostly, human beings are the only ones responsible for all activities, actions and events which occur in those spaces, where a person controls not only his/her body but also vehicles such as cars, bikes or heavy equipments. In this dissertation, "*object*" is employed to indicate a human being or its vehicles.

The variation of objects reflects on their capabilities and competences, based on which they are able to perform lots of activities. An activity can be literally defined as "*something that people do or cause to happen.*" [Web]. Specifically, in computer vision, activities are categorised in terms of their complexity levels. Namely, the categories from the lowest to the highest levels are: gesture, actions, interaction, group activities and behaviours [BCC13; AR11]. Gestures are the basic movements of body parts, which describe the local motion of a person (e.g., stretching hand). Moreover, temporally organised gestures are considered as atomic components of an action, representing voluntary body movements such as "walking" or "jumping". Interactions are formed by two or more actions, where each action is the reaction of its predecessor (e.g., brawl). Unlike interactions, group activities are performed by multiple objects sharing the action such as people walking together in a group. Behaviours are the activities which describe the intentions behind the activities of the lower-level categories. For example, the action of "walking" may lead to different behaviours: "thieving", "crossing road", etc.

In addition to the categories of activities, Figure 1.1 illustrates a brief taxonomy of most used feature types, video types, learning methods and approaches to analyse the activities discussed above. In general, the type of a video is an important cue to follow a suitable framework for analysing given activities. The reason is that the video type implies the

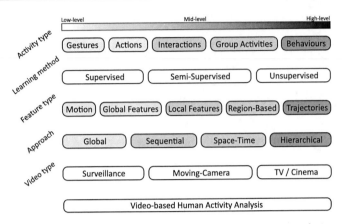

Figure 1.1: A general taxonomy of video-based human activity analysis.

processing complexity. For example, surveillance videos are complex in terms of object resolution [GA+12], while the challenge of videos from moving camera lies in the difference of coordinate systems [WOS11]. Depending on the desired activities to be analysed, the types of feature and approach are defined, where they both also differ in their complexity levels. Global approaches consider a video as a single block, where it can be represented by a set of low-level features such as the dense optical flow [Wan+11; WS13]. On the contrary, the sequential approach considers the continuous changes along frames, by extracting global features such as texture [Cro+08] or local features such as Scale-Invariant Feature Transform (SIFT) [SAS07]. Using global and sequential approaches, only low-level activities (i.e., gestures and actions) can be analysed. As for higher level activities, spatio-temporal approaches [Dol+05; KS13; YT14] are widely used, where features are analysed in the chronological order based on their temporal positions. For this, specific regions such as body parts, ground plane, etc. can be employed, where they are determined based on lower-level features (e.g., Histograms of Oriented Gradients (HOG), SIFT, etc). The sequential positions of those regions called "trajectories" are considered as the highest level features which can characterise high-level activities [MT08; PMF08]. Finally, hierarchical approaches [Dai+08; RA09] focus on detecting high-level activities based on lower-level ones, called "sub-events" or "atomic activities". For example a *cooking* activity can be recognised by considering other activities such as *stretching hand* and *stationary position* [Roh+16].

Basically, the difficulty of video-based human activity analysis lies in the fact that the extracted features of different activities have high inter-class similarity, especially for high-level cases. For example, the distinction between "soccer" and "hand-ball" games is complex because both enclose almost the same atomic actions. Therefore, activities can be learned and classified based on their features using different learning methods. For the activities that are well determined (e.g., eating, cooking, etc), a supervised method can be used [MT08]. A semi-supervised method is mainly employed when the data are partially labelled or only a part of the activities is defined (e.g., abnormality cases) [Wan+14]. In the scenario where activities are hard to be defined, an unsupervised method [WMG09] is more suitable due to its ability of dispensing with the annotation process.

Due to the enormous number of activity patterns that can be detected and analysed, this dissertation focuses on automatically analysing the activities which arise from objects mobilities. In other words, the activities that can be expressed by the sequential positions (trajectories) of objects. More specifically, this work aims to detect convoys (moving together patterns) and suspicious activities, which are essential patterns being fraught with valuable information and can pretend undesirable consequences [Zhe15].

1.1 Problem

Analysing and detecting object activities is a challenging task, since objects have plenty of freedom regarding performing actions, which in turn yield complex activities. Besides, a concrete analysis of activities needs high-level information, which cannot be readily available. For example, an activity of two persons walking together is entirely different from one person following another, both in terms of behaviours and consequences. However, it is not easy to distinguish between these activities without understanding the relationship between individuals. Another example, pickpocketing is an activity that requires a high accuracy of observation, so that it can be detected in real time. For this, it is assumed that every activity that occurs in public spaces is preceded by a mobility expressing its nature. Precisely, people likely keep a small distance between them while walking together. Pickpocket thieves have neither a clear target nor a stable path. Consequently, it is proposed in this dissertation to study the 3D trajectories of objects which represent high-level semantic features. Here, a 3D trajectory of a given object means its sequential positions in the real world. The aim is to automatically understand object-activities in different kinds of videos, assuming that the trajectory of an object implies its current, elapsed or starting activity.

Recently, objects become inseparable from trackable devices (e.g., smartphones, wearables, Global Positioning System (GPS) devices for cars, etc.), with which their trajectories can be easily extracted. However, accessing to those devices may face with many technical and ethical obstacles. In addition to the privacy violation, people may disable their tracking devices to accomplish unacceptable activities indistinctly. Here, it is necessary to rely on external sensors that are able to extract the 3D trajectories of objects and protect their privacy simultaneously. Among few sensors which ensure the extraction of those trajectories, multi-cameras can be employed to accurately localising multiple objects in their 3D positions. In addition to perceiving depth, multi-cameras are capable of overcoming the occlusion since objects are captured from different perspectives. However, the employment of these cameras incurs a high calibration cost. On the contrary, depth cameras are cheap and easy to use, in addition to their high accuracy. Despite their advantages, the restrictions of depth cameras (e.g., small depth range, disable outdoor) make their performance very limited. Therefore, the generality of the approach is ensured by using monocular cameras, which are cheap, easy to use and do not require a calibration process. For the sake of brevity, the terminology is abused in this dissertation by referring to videos that are taken from monocular cameras as "monocular videos". Similarly, videos taken from uncalibrated and/or moving cameras are referred as "uncalibrated and/or moving videos".

The challenge of extracting 3D trajectories of objects from monocular videos lies on several difficulties. The first is detecting objects in still images, where objects are characterised by diverse visual appearances. In such a situation, it needs an expensive computational cost to exhaustively search all possible regions in a frame for finding target objects. To overcome this deficiency, it is necessary to carefully search the least possible regions that are more likely to contain objects. The second is the freedom of objects' movements, which cause a huge variety of their appearances and make the estimation of their 3D positions more complex. More precisely, object appearances (e.g., colour, shape, etc.) are usually unstable in videos, since objects in the same category can appear in different formats based on the angle of view. Moreover, one object can change its appearance from frame to another because most intended objects have deformable characteristics. Furthermore, the high occlusion, especially in crowded environments, makes the total reliance on visual tracking unavailing, and thus the position prediction of an occluded object becomes an urgent need to solve the problem. However, even if objects move systematically in the space, they do not follow clear paths all the time due to the obstacles or the complex relations between them, where an object can suddenly change the relationship with other objects any time. For example, a person can move alone, then meet other people, and then enter to his/her car. Another essential problem of monocular cameras is the lack of depth information, which does not allow to estimate object positions on the longitudinal axis. For this reason, the problem of extracting 3D trajectories of objects from 2D video can be solved by adopting a probabilistic approach, due to its flexibility and the potential integration of multiple cues.

For more general scenarios, this work considers both videos, already recorded (e.g., Internet videos) and those taken from moving cameras, which can be used to capture public spaces (e.g., surveillance). The characteristic of these videos presents another challenge because, in addition to the lack of depth, neither the camera parameters nor scene knowledge is assumed to be available. Practically, the camera movement is measured by studying the relation between the real world and the image plane. This relation is governed by several factors such as the focal length of the camera, the depths of captured points and the resolution of the image. All of these factors are necessary in order to correctly project points from the real world to the image plane and vice versa. For this, it is proposed to use available cues in order to estimate the missing information.

Using trajectories to detect and analyse object activities is another serious problem, where in addition to the freedom of movements, objects behave according to many external and internal factors such as the place, the target destination and the crowd density. For example, people eschew in their movements stationary people gatherings [YLW15b]. Also, such activities cannot be characterised by specific properties, where it is not practical to predefine all possible achievable activities. Moreover, the same internal properties of an activity under specific conditions do not yield the same activity under different conditions. For example, a car driving $120km/h$ is absolutely a normal activity on the high way, but the same speed is considered as a highly risky activity if it happened in the city. In addition to the complexity of characterising some activity types (especially the unusual ones), it is difficult to consider all conditions in order to define their natures. Therefore, it is proposed in this dissertation to learn the activity types from the completed ones automatically. Furthermore, analysing group activities based on objects' trajectories faces with the difficulty of understanding the complex relationships between the objects, which change their intra properties (e.g., relative positions of objects in one group) and inter properties (e.g., a group can cross another group). Therefore, this problem can be solved by continuously studying the relation between objects over time.

1.2 Contribution

The contributions of this work are dedicated to overcoming the above mentioned problems, where a complete framework system is proposed. Figure 1.2 illustrates the pipeline of the trajectory-based human activity analysis framework. Here, the first aim is to detect objects (e.g., people and cars) in still images. Secondly, extracting objects trajectories in the real world from stationary and moving 2D videos. The final goal is to use the extracted trajectories to detect two activity patterns: (1) group activities called *convoy patterns*, which can gather two or more pedestrians moving or standing together as one pattern. (2) suspicious activities that may happen in public spaces. To address the goals of this work, the

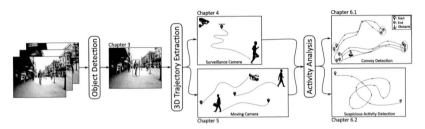

Figure 1.2: The pipeline of the proposed framework for trajectory-based human activity analysis.

contributions are given in a short summary as follows:

Object Detection: Objects are the vital elements in videos, producing different kinds of activities. Therefore, two methods are developed to detect those objects in crowded scenes initially. The first method considers the object as a set of moving key-points. Therefore, it is practical to detect known objects in surveillance videos. The second method is more general, where it learns deep features from examples to detect different kinds of objects in different types of image.

3D Trajectory Extraction from Stationary Camera: 3D trajectory of an object denotes its sequential position in the 3D space over time. One approach [Bou+15a] to extract those trajectories from 2D videos is to combine object detection [Fel+10] and depth estimation [KLK16], which are performed on each frame in a video. Using particle filtering [Aru+02], the detected objects are tracked in the image plane and then converted into the real world.

Simultaneous 3D Trajectory Extraction from Moving Camera: To extract 3D trajectories from more complicated videos, another contribution of this work is to simultaneously extract 3D trajectories of both the objects and the camera. This sub-framework consists of several methods that can also be independently used for other applications. First, since the intrinsic parameters of the camera are not supposed to be provided, the focal length is estimated. The proposed method is effective even when the geometrical features are not available. Another contribution is devoted to estimating the depths of detected objects in order to compensate the lack of depth information in 2D videos. Finally, Reversible Jump Markov Chain Monte Carlo (RJ-MCMC) particle filtering is used with the support of robust observation cues to simultaneously localise the camera and multiple objects in the real world. Assuming similar examples should have comparable characteristics, the proposed tracking method makes use of examples in order to estimate the missing information. This is used to relax the restrictions, and thus it can be applied to different kind of videos.

Convoy Detection: The detection of group activities is crucial in crowd activity analysis. Consequently, a robust convoy detection method is proposed in this dissertation by analysing the trajectories of objects.

Suspicious Activity Detection: Due to their importance, suspicious activities are recognised in the crowd, assuming that they occur rarely compared to normal ones. For this, objects' trajectories are considered as valuable features, being able to distinguish between normal and suspicious activities.

1.3 Overview

The underlying dissertation is organised into eight chapters, where **Chapter 2** introduces an overview of existing works in order to understand the novelty of this work. Moreover, the next four chapters present the contribution corresponding to the structure of **Chapter 2**, where each chapter denotes a sub-project, whose output is the input of the subsequent chapters. However, each sub-project can be separately used for different applications. A brief description of those chapters is given as follows:

Chapter 3 describes two proposed methods of objects detection, where the first one is mainly used to detect pedestrians from videos that are taken from a stationary camera. The second is more general and can be used to detect different kinds of objects in images.

Chapter 4 introduces a new method to extract 3D trajectories of objects from 2D surveillance videos. Here, an explanation of initialising an object in the real world is given. After that, the estimation of the sequential positions of the object is discussed.

Chapter 5 presents a sub-framework for extracting 3D trajectories of the objects and the camera. First, a focal length estimation method is presented, followed by object-based depth estimation method. Then, it describes a modified RJ-MCMC particle filtering that sequentially estimates the positions of objects, including the camera.

Chapter 6 proposes two applications of analysing object activities using their trajectories. Both applications focus on analysing activities in the crowd, where the first detects convoys and the second recognises suspicious activities.

The remaining chapters are dedicated to validate the proposed methods and conclude the discussion. Specifically, **Chapter 7** follows the same general structure to evaluate each method and sub-method, whose results are confirmed using challenging datasets. However, it has to be noted that although each method is considered as a vital phase in the generic framework, its result is not necessarily used in the evaluation of the subsequent phases. Finally, **Chapter 8** summarises the observations that have drawn attention to improving this work. Consequently, the dissertation is closed with a discussion about possible further directions to extend and open new future research tasks.

Chapter 2

Related Work

This chapter comprises a literature review of relevant work and presents it based on its similarity to the presented methods. Section 2.1 surveys related approaches of object detection. Subsequently, an overview of the most related methods in tracking and trajectory extraction is presented in Section 2.2. Section 2.3 then reviews several methods that estimate internal and external camera parameters including camera odometry. Finally, the approaches that address the use of trajectories in activity analyses are presented in Section 2.4.

2.1 Object Detection

Detecting objects in Red-Green-Blue (RGB) images is fundamental in computer vision, as it is important in several applications such as video surveillance, scene understanding and object tracking. For this reason, it is a topic that has been addressed by researchers for a long period of time. Thus, extant work related to object detection is divided into the following three categories: segmentation, exhaustive search and superficial search.

2.1.1 Segmentation

Since the projection of objects onto an image plane creates a significant disparity between the foreground and the background, several methods [EH14; CS10a] take advantage of this characteristic by segmenting the foreground from the background, in which the foreground segment is considered to form the object (complete or partial). Endres and Hoiem [EH14] have proposed to automatically generate a small number of regions in an image based on estimated boundaries, geometry, colour and texture, assuming that each object is well-represented by at least one region. Afterwards, a structured learning approach is used to rank the generated regions so that the top-ranked regions are likely to correspond to different objects.

Gu *et al.* [Gu+09] consider regions that may contain object's parts to be the primary elements of their approach. First, an image is represented as a bag of regions, each of which is described by its colour, shape and texture features. Second, hypotheses concerning the object's location, scale and support are generated based on region-grouping after determining each region's weight using a discriminative max-margin framework.

2.1.2   Exhaustive Search

Practically, an object can be located at any position having any size scale on the image plane. Therefore, early approaches find it logical to search everywhere and for every scale to detect and recognise objects [VJ04; DT05; HJS09]. However, the vastness of the visual search space makes the computational cost extremely high. Otherwise, the number of considered locations would be less and hence decreased precision. In this endeavour, several techniques search for objects using a coarse sliding window that has a fixed aspect ratio, which adopts lower level features, such as HOG. These features are then classified using a series of classifiers, such as Support Vector Machine (SVM) [CV95]. Felzenszwalb *et al.* [Fel+10] have proposed a deformable, part-based object detection method that exhaustively searches for objects and object parts using HOG features and a linear SVM.

Another method proposed by Lampert *et al.* [LBH09] guides the search using the appearance model, which in addition to reducing the number of visited locations, tolerates different aspect ratios and scales of the searching window. Precisely, the method searches for optimal windows in the image using a branch and bound technique, and subsequently, uses a linear classifier to discard non-object regions and classify the remaining ones.

2.1.3   Superficial Search

Recent works in object detection have proposed to reduce the number of visited locations and to search for objects with different scales and aspect ratios. The challenge here is maintaining the same level of accuracy and computation costs with fewer candidate regions that are various sizes and with different aspect ratios. Alexe *et al.* [ADF12] have randomly generated windows that are classified using an object classifier, which is trained for familiar shape objects (e.g., pedestrian, car, etc.). Subsequently, the "objectness" measurement performed by the classifier is used to reduce the number of windows (object hypotheses) evaluated by the object detectors.

Vedaldi *et al.* [Ved+09] have also addressed the problem of reducing the number of object hypotheses by predicting all possible object locations. Their method learns to predict the object's location by studying the relation between individual visual words and object locations in training images. Furthermore, Maji and Malik [MBM08] have considered more complex relationships to predict object location using a Hough-transform [DH72]. Another method, proposed by Uijlings *et al.* [Uij+13], selectively searches for object locations, scales and aspect ratios by hierarchically grouping small segmented regions.

2.2 Trajectory Extraction

Many research studies have been conducted to extract trajectories from visual sequences with a difference in the adoption of the coordinate system. Tracking specific regions in the image coordinate system is also considered for trajectory extraction. This is possible if the camera setup fulfils the necessary conditions, such as the total stability of the intrinsic and extrinsic camera parameters. Moreover, the camera position should ensure high parallel relativity between the image plane and the ground plane in the camera coordinates. Thus, the development of the objects' positions on the image plane does not significantly deviate from their real movements on the ground plane. For this purpose, surveillance cameras are arranged in a suitable way to monitor objects moving on the ground stably.

For other applications, objects positions on an image coordinate system are not valuable due to their lack of metric information. Consequently, another approach direction is to project objects from the image plane onto the world coordinate system [HEH08] to place them in a real world perspective and extract their 3D trajectories. Here, the availability of some or many parameters (e.g., focal length, camera height, object's depth and object's size) is necessary to determine the relation between the image plane and the real world. Furthermore, moving cameras are used to explore the environment and its content of objects. Simply projecting objects' regions from the image plane into the real world over an image sequence does not yield the extraction of 3D trajectories of the objects. Rather, the extraction of their positions w.r.t the camera position, which changes over time. The following presents and discusses the extant work regarding tracking objects and extracting their 3D trajectories from both stationary and moving videos.

2.2.1 3D Object Tracking

The racking objects and regions in video sequences can be divided into three categories: matching-based tracking, filtering-based tracking and fusion-based tracking [Men+15]. This section discusses each of these categories in detail.

2.2.1.1   Matching-based Tracking

Considering that objects are detected at each frame, the tracking problem is formulated as making the correspondence of those detections over frames. The method proposed by Jepson *et al.* [JFEM01] is supposed to be robust against occlusion. This approach results in the best match between the region template and all possible locations in the target frame. The matching is computed using an adaptive appearance model, based on texture features. Furthermore, the object model is updated during tracking using an online Expectation-Maximisation (EM) algorithm [DLR77]. The method proposed by Tissainayagam *et al.* [TS05] tracks the local maximum corner points (key points) that define an object. Although the presented results are accurate, their method is not robust for objects that have deformable characteristics or a smooth texture. Yilmaz *et al.* [XLS04] have addressed this problem by proposing to guide tracking using kernel density estimation and the Gabor wavelet model based on the colour feature and texture feature, respectively.

2.2.1.2   Filtering-based Tracking

The systematic movements of objects have caused researchers to consider such movements as cues in object tracking, which is formulated as a state estimation problem. The Kalman filter [Bas01; MS83; Nor04; JU04] is widely used for state prediction, by estimating the posterior probability density function. However, large perturbation in objects' movements makes the Kalman filter ineffective. The Particle filter [GSS93] is a sequential Monte Carlo filter, which is used to solve non-linear, non-Gaussian Bayesian estimation problems, and was first introduced and applied to visual tracking by Isard and Blake [IB98]. Since then, the particle filter was vastly used for visual tracking [Bao+12; JF10; Lee+05; Li+12; Ros+08; Kwo+14]. For example, Kwon *et al.* [Kwo+14] have exhibited the effectiveness of particle filtering for projective motion tracking that does not require vector parametrization of the homographies.

2.2.1.3   Fusion-based Tracking

Since each tracking algorithm has its own strengths and weakness, another direction is to combine two or more algorithms to take advantage of the different methods and thus, obtain more accurate tracking results [Heb+13; STW07]. Shan *et al.* [STW07] have proposed a Mean Shift (MS) embedded particle filter algorithm, which overcomes the degeneracy problem and improves the sampling efficiency by requiring fewer particles to maintain multiple hypotheses, hence achieving a low computational cost.

2.2.2 3D Trajectory Extraction from Surveillance Videos

Existing methods for extracting 3D trajectories from 2D videos can be classified into two categories: multi-cues and mapping-based.

2.2.2.1 Multi-cues

Using multiple views of a scene, objects can be accurately localised in 3D space and be placed in perspective [Gar+13; SMO05; Zha+15; Mor+14]. For example, the method proposed by Morais *et al.*[Mor+14] exhibits promising results (error average $< 70cm$) by adopting multiple cameras and using particle filter to track futsal players. However, accurately localising objects in 3D space using multiple cameras necessitates extra processes of calibration and pixel correspondences and thus, requires a high computational cost. On the other hand, depth cameras (e.g., Kinect) provide better results in terms of depth accuracy and are less complex regarding adjustment with RGB image. In this case, the depth not only increases the accuracy of the tracking process but also solves other problems such as occlusion and object misdetection. Respectively, many studies have used this sensor [SX13; JML14; CWL15]. For example, the method by Song *et al.*[SX13] associates objects' regions that are detected using Red-Green-Blue Depth (RGB-D), HOG features and Hosseini *et al.*[JML14] have proposed to use two different detectors for different distance ranges: a fast depth-based upper-body detector for close range and an appearance-based full-body HOG detector for farther distances. Since depth sensors provide prepared depth maps contrary to multi-view sensors, their system can run online (20 frames per second (fps)).

2.2.2.2 Mapping-based

The majority of methods that localise objects in 3D space using a monocular RGB camera assume a prior knowledge of the relation between the image plane and the real world. Therefore, some camera parameters (e.g., focal length, camera height, etc) must be available, and a site-map is partially known to place objects in perspective. Song *et al.* [SM14] assume that the camera focal length is available, with which the translation and rotation are estimated. Since the metric information is missing, the translation is ambiguous with a scale factor, which is corrected by estimating the height and orientation of the ground plane relative to the camera. Assuming that all objects move on the same ground plane as the camera w.r.t its height, they can be projected from the image plane to the 3D space and vice-versa.

It is currently still difficult to set multiple cameras for ordinary usage since they require calibration and a certain stability between cameras. Similarly, many conditions must be satisfied for 3D (e.g., indoor, limited depth range, etc.), making it impractical in real scenarios. Assumptions, such as focal length and camera rotation allow the use of a monocular camera, however, in real scenarios most videos are recorded from a monocular camera without providing its parameters.

2.2.3   3D Trajectory Extraction from Moving Cameras

Extracting the 3D trajectories of objects has been addressed by many researchers [CPS13; CS10b; Woj+11; Woj+13; Xia+14; Ess+09]. To understand traffic scenes, the framework proposed by Wojek *et al.* [Woj+11; Woj+13] combines multiple detectors for estimating the trajectories of multiple objects from moving videos. Furthermore, Ess *et al.* [Ess+09] have proposed a probabilistic approach that simultaneously estimates the positions of multiple objects and the camera by combining several detectors. The method proposed by Choi *et al.* [CPS13; CS10b] similarly localises the camera multiple acquired pedestrians in the real world without referring to depth information, where a more sophisticated probabilistic approach is adopted to analyse the interaction between moving objects. This approach called RJ-MCMC particle filtering was introduced by Khan *et al.* [KBD05] in order to simultaneously track multiple interacting targets. Here, the aim is to estimate the whole probability distribution with fewer samples in order to reduce the computational cost. For this, a novel Markov Chain Monte Carlo (MCMC) sampling step is adopted instead of employing the traditional importance sampling step in the particle filtering. Moreover, the complexity of targets' interaction is handled by incorporating Markov Random Field (MRF) to model those interactions.

2.3   Camera Parameters Estimation

The relation between the real world and the image plane is controlled by the intrinsic camera parameters, in case the camera is stationary. On the contrary, both intrinsic and extrinsic parameters are responsible for determining this relationship. The intrinsic parameters are the characteristics of the camera that make it possible to project each point in the world coordinate system onto the image plane. Precisely, they denote the principal points (very close to image centres), the skew parameter (mostly ≈ 0) and the focal length, as can be seen in Figure 2.1, where the focal length is considered the most crucial parameter affecting the projection. The extrinsic parameters represent the geometric transformation (rotation and translation) of the camera in the real world, as shown in Figure 2.2. In the following, existing approaches that estimate the camera focal length and its localisation are presented.

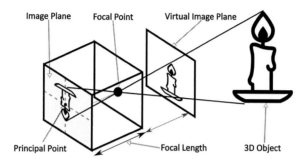

Figure 2.1: A general overview of the intrinsic camera parameters.

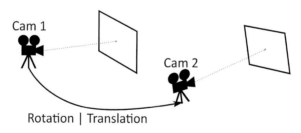

Figure 2.2: A general overview of the extrinsic camera parameters: Rotation and Translation between two cameras (Cam 1 & Cam 2).

2.3.1   Focal Length Estimation

The focal length of the camera helps understand the relation between the image plane and the 3D space and make correspondences between 2D and 3D points. Penate-Sanchez *et al.* [PSACMN13] have proposed a non-minimal method known *Exhaustive Linearisation* that inversely retrieves camera focal length from 2D-to-3D correspondences by circumventing the limitations of the current linearisation-based approaches. Furthermore, Workman *et al.* [Wor+15] have directly estimated the focal length using only raw pixel intensities as the input features by investigating the application of a deep convolutional neural network. The idea is to update the final fully-connected layer of *AlexNet* to establish a single output node corresponding to the horizontal field of view, which needs to be estimated. Another approach proposed by Sattler *et al.* [SSP14] estimates the focal length by sampling from a discrete set of possible values. Precisely, a RANSAC variant called "P3P(f)-RANSAC" has been proposed, where in each iteration, a focal length value is randomly selected based on the probability of finding a better model for it, which is computed using a recursive Bayesian filter.

2.3.2   Camera Odometry Estimation

Estimating camera motion (camera odometry) has long drawn the attention of researchers due to its importance in an enormous number of applications such as autonomous driving and robotics. As previously described, camera odometry can be achieved using either multi cues (e.g., stereo camera) or mono cue (e.g., monocular camera) sensors:

2.3.2.1   Multi-cues

For an accurate camera pose estimation, the most important cue (in addition to the RGB image sequence) is depth information. Therefore, a large study was conducted using RGB-D cameras [GGMCG15; KSC13; Han+14; JGJ15; ZK15; Nar+15]. For example Gutiérrez-Gómez *et al.* [GGMCG15] have proposed a fast visual odometry method (100 Hz) that uses Graphics Processing Unit (GPU)s based on the alignment between consecutive frames. The key here is to minimise both photometric and geometric errors, which are parametrised using inverse depth. Whelan *et al.* [Whe+15] have presented a real-time method that corrects the dense map according to place recognition by extending the dense, every-frame volumetric fusion and combining geometric and photometric camera pose constraints to cover a wide variety of environments. Despite the high accuracy of RGB-D-based camera odometry, it does not work in outdoor environments due to the limited capability of depth sensors.

Stereo-cameras can provide depth information under harsher conditions including outdoor environments. For this reason, they were considered in several studies [CP15; BW16; Per+15; Zha+15]. For example, Cvišić *et al.* [CP15] have proposed to track stable features after a careful selection, and then separately estimate the rotation using the five-point method, whereas the translation is estimated using the three-point method. Persson *et al.* [Per+15] have proposed a method that generalises monocular-based odometry techniques to the stereo case, achieving significant improvement in both the robustness and accuracy of stereo-based odometry.

2.3.2.2 Mono-cue

Another research direction of reducing the global cost is to consider using a monocular camera, which is cheap, easy to use and does not need a calibration process [MM15; SM14; MM14; GZS11; FKM16]. Mirabdollah and Mertsching [MM15] have proposed a fast technique for real-time monocular-based camera odometry using the five-point method within a RANdom SAmple Consensus (RANSAC) scheme. For this purpose, they localised landmarks in the space using multiple observations that are resulting from a probabilistic triangulation method. Moreover, they minimise a cost function that consists of epipolar geometry constraints for far landmarks and projective constraints for those that are near. Song and Chandraker [SM14] have presented a framework that corrects the scale drift and estimates ground plane by combining object bounding box detection, dense inter-frame stereo, spare features and learning models from a training dataset. Moreover, Engel *et al.*[ESC13] have proposed a new featureless method to track the motion of a camera using dense image alignment after estimating the semi-dense inverse depth map, which represents the depth of all pixels with a non-negligible image gradient.

In view of the state-of-the-art methods, it is important to note that in spite of their high accuracy, they are incapable of dealing with all uncalibrated monocular videos without assistance. In other words, mono cue approaches are usually supported with 3D information such as admitted key-points with known relation to the camera (e.g., points on the ground plane). Otherwise, they depend on learning from training examples or models.

2.4 Trajectory Analysis

Trajectory analysis is a key research area in machine learning and data mining. The aim is to interpret trajectories, obtained by different devices, to concrete activities. Due to the largeness of this research area, this section reviews methods and approaches that are related to the detection of convoys and suspicious activities based on trajectories.

2.4.1   Convoy Detection

The detection and estimation of crowd motion patterns have been widely studied

Detecting and estimating crowd motion patterns have been largely used [WMG09; Sha+15; ZWT12] with the aim of modelling and understanding pedestrian interactions. Using the same approach, another study has addressed the problem of studying normal crowd behaviours [SMS12] (e.g., bottlenecks, lanes and blocking) and abnormal ones [MOS09; Mah+10], by considering psychological and physical effects.

Recently, researchers have considered group activities to be an important cue in understanding and analysing crowded scenes. For example, Shao *et al.* [SLW14] have used motion pattern estimation to detect, characterise and quantify group properties (e.g., uniformity, conflict,etc) in a crowded scene. This method is based on identifying an anchor tracklet for every group, which can be selected based on its continuous existence in the scene. Thus, several further frames need to be processed, and therefore the method cannot run sequentially (online). Many other methods analyse mobile social groups based on the relative distances and velocities of moving pedestrians [GCR12; CKG11; Lan+12; AT11], however, they ignore stationary crowd groups.

On the other hand, other studies have demonstrated the high impact of stationary groups on the changing traffic properties of crowded and non-crowded scenes [Mou+10; YLW15a; Yi+14; YLW15b]. In [Mou+10; YLW15b], researchers consider that stationary groups significantly influence the walking path of other moving pedestrians, counter to moving groups which can influence the velocities of other moving pedestrians. Moreover, Yi *et al.* [YLW15a; Yi+14] have revealed the impact of stationary groups on the travel time of a pedestrian from his/her entrance onto the scene until his/her exit.

2.4.2   Suspicious Activity Detection

Several methods have been developed to detect suspicious activities in surveillance videos, specifically in crowded scenes[GS15; Li+15; KN09; LSL14; Lee+15; HZD13; WZL16]. The majority of existing methods assume that normal activities are performed by the majority of people and that abnormal ones occur rarely. Therefore, these methods propose to use unsupervised learning approaches for this detection. For example, Hu *et al* [HZD13] have detected abnormal activities without the need of training examples by scanning the video using a large number of windows, where each window is compared with its surroundings. Wang *et al.* [WZL16] have proposed to detect spatio-temporal visual saliency based on the phase spectrum of the video. Despite the high accuracy of the visual motion-based methods, they cannot accurately localise an abnormality in the scene, since the coherence of the background can be violated by any other unexpected object (e.g., a bird) or if rotating surveillance cameras are used. On the other hand, analysing the trajectories can detect, localise and identify the offending abnormal activity, regardless of the source of those trajectories [GFH16; MT11; Cos+17]. For example, Ghrab *et al.* [GFH16] have proposed a two phase method, where in the first phase, the training activities are clustered offline using an agglomerative hierarchical approach and in the second phase, the extracted trajectories are associated with the clusters relying on the distance similarity. Although the presented methods are exceedingly accurate, they rely either on fully labelled training data or completely unlabelled examples and thus, the first approach requires a substantial amount of manual work for each scenario, while the second one is not robust with complex trajectories.

Chapter 3

Object Detection

This chapter discusses the initial process of object tracking and activity analysis, which is dedicated to recognise the existence of objects. The automatic detection of objects in images is one of the fundamental challenges in computer vision, due to the different shapes, colours and poses in their appearances. It is supposed to be very easy for human beings to detect objects from images and videos with naked eyes, even with low resolution. However, this is only possible if some conditions are satisfied such as a surrounding visibility. Figure 3.1 shows a clear example of the importance of the surrounding to recognise low-resolution objects, where as shown in the left side the image can be easily understood. On the contrary, the black car is difficult to be recognised in the right side due to the absence of the surrounding.

Figure 3.1: An example of the difficulty of recognising a low-resolution object by human beings without the surrounding environment.

Especially in surveillance videos, objects do not appear in a way that classical object detectors can detect, which is due to the particular setup of these cameras. Specifically, surveillance cameras are installed to capture wide views, so that many objects are monitored and tracked for a long duration. Additionally, their resulting videos have low resolution to reduce the required storage space. Since a part of this work is addressed to the problem of analysing objects' activities from surveillance videos, in the following, two methods to detect pedestrians from surveillance videos are proposed.

3.1   Object Detection in Surveillance Videos

The main difficulty of detecting objects in crowded videos is the low resolution, where different objects may have similar appearances such as a tree and a person. However, the projection of most of the objects can be easily distinguished from the background in terms of colour and texture continuities, regardless of the resolution. In such a situation, extracted key-point can describe the sudden changes in the colour and the texture of the image, assuming that objects' regions contain a sufficient number of key-points [Bou+16a]. Therefore, the proposed method detects objects by clustering feature points as illustrated in Figure 3.2. To determine Region-Of-Interest (ROI)s of objects from the background, corner and edge detection are applied. For this, canny edge detection [Can86] is proposed due to its proved performance [GS12]. Moreover, this method is extended to improve the clustering process in the subsequent frames, by adding a new criterion about key-points' displacements. In the following the clustering in the first frame and its improvement are explained:

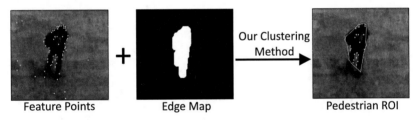

Figure 3.2: An overview of the proposed pedestrian detection method using key-points.

3.1.1   Clustering for One Frame

Usually, the projection of objects such as pedestrians causes a significant discontinuity in the spatial characteristics of the image. This property can be used to distinguish objects from the background. Consequently, key-points called *Features from Accelerated Segment Test (FAST)* are extracted using [RD06], which is known as a fast corner detection method outputting a set of feature points. In addition to separating objects from the background, the sensitivity of FAST method allows detecting key-points inside objects' ROIs. To balance this sensitivity, detected edges are a good cue to show the details of the image and delineate objects. The ROI of an object is assumed to be entirely traced by a closed boundary or inside a big closed boundary. Given an image im, $\mathbf{r} = \{r_1, r_2, \ldots, r_n\}$ is the set of extracted key-points, and C is the corresponding canny edge map. Algorithm 1 summarises the process of determining the set of clusters $\mathbf{c}$, each of which represents object's ROI.

Algorithm 1: Clustering algorithm (r)

---

1   **while** $\mathbf{r} \neq \emptyset$ **do**

2   Select an anchor a^i point from $\mathbf{r}$ to define a new cluster $\mathbf{c}^i$;

3    $\mathbf{r} = \mathbf{r} \setminus a^i$;

4   Select from $\mathbf{r}$ a set of feature points $\mathbf{b}^i$ satisfying clustering criteria;

5   **if** $\mathbf{b}^i \neq \emptyset$ **then**

6   Assign $\mathbf{b}^i$ to $\mathbf{c}^i$;

7      $\mathbf{r} = \mathbf{r} \setminus \mathbf{b}^i$;

In each iteration, the above algorithm selects an anchor point from the set of non-clustered extracted key-points $\mathbf{r}$. The chosen point is the one having the highest number of neighbours with the lowest average distance. In other words, the anchor point is the centre of a dense region of key-point. The clustering process is completed by assigning the neighbours to a^i, where they must be inside the same closed edge. As illustrated in Figure 3.2, the key-points inside the region that define the pedestrian are merged into one cluster. In addition, the probable size of the object's bounding box is priorly set to guide the clustering process. To this end, the key-points are restricted to form bounding-boxes with the maximum threshold α and β denoting the maximum object height and width, respectively.

3.1.2 Clustering Improvement for a Frame Sequence

For subsequent frames in the sequence, another cue can be involved to improve the detection, where in still images key-points are detected in all over the frame including the background (non-object regions). Therefore, this cue is used to discard false positive clusters. In surveillance cameras, motions are exceptionally made by moving objects due to the stability of the camera, where stationary pixels are assumed to represent the background and moving ones represent objects. Even stationary pedestrians cannot avoid moving locally in the small region which they occupy [YLW15a]. The idea is to consider only key-points which appear in im_t and im_{t-1} and neglect those which cannot be tracked [Bou+16a]. For this, additional SIFT-based key-points $\mathbf{s} = \{s_1, s_2, .., s_{n'}\}$ are extracted from im_t using the open source library

VLFeat [VF08]. Since a huge number of SIFT Keypoints can be extracted covering the whole image, the final set of feature points of im_t is $\mathbf{l} = \mathbf{r} \cap \mathbf{s}$. Similarly to im_t, a set of SIFT key-points denoted as $\mathbf{l}^\circ$ is extracted from im_{t-1}, where both sets are matched by finding the closest point descriptors in im_t to those in im_{t-1}. This characterisation of measuring the velocity and the direction of each point in $\mathbf{l}^\circ$ to its correspondent in $\mathbf{l}$ is done by the L2 norm of the difference between them [VF08]. As a result, a set is obtained, consisting of key-points which are likely to characterise moving and stationary pedestrians in the scene.

Finally, Algorithm 1 is followed in order to cluster the set of key-points $\mathbf{l}$ into pedestrian regions by adapting it with a new criterion. Here, key-points are assigned to the cluster defined by the anchor point based on their movements, where they must have similar velocity and direction. Moreover, clusters with velocity $\simeq 0$ are supposed to belong to non-object regions, and thus they are neglected.

3.2   Object Detection in Still Images

In more complicated scenarios, it is difficult to detect objects using the method presented in 3.1. Here, a complex scenario means a situation where external motions appear in the scene in addition to those of moving objects. Explicitly, the method described in 3.1 considers any block of motion flow, which fulfils certain conditions as a moving object. This approach is ineffective when there is a motion collision (e.g., rotating surveillance cameras) or different kinds of objects in the scene having various sizes (e.g., cars and people). For this, a method is proposed to effectively detect objects regardless their sizes or categories. Given a query image, Figure 3.3 illustrates the pipeline of the proposed detection method. First, a systematic search is performed to the whole frame in order to extract all possible candidate regions that may contain objects. Using Caffe framework [Jia+14], each candidate image is encoded as a semantic feature vector extracted from the **fc7** layer (4096-dimensions) of VggNet-16[SZ14][1]. Features extracted from this layer are assumed to describe high-level semantic content of a given image. Since only one object category (i.e., pedestrian) is considered, extracted candidate regions are classified into positive (pedestrian) and negative (non-pedestrian) using a pre-trained linear SVM-Model. Given all positive candidates, overlapped ones are merged based on their overlap proportions and classification confidence scores, where the remaining with low scores are discarded. Each process in the detection method is explained below:

---

[1]http://www.robots.ox.ac.uk/~vgg/research/very_deep/

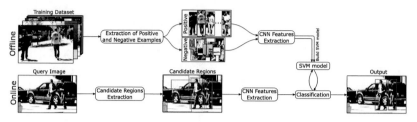

Figure 3.3: An overview of the proposed object detection method using Convolutional Neural Network (CNN)-based features.

3.2.1 Systematic Search

In order to extract candidates which are more likely to contain objects regions, locations of possible object candidates are searched by hierarchically grouping regions following [Uij+13]. The image is first divided into small sub-regions of same sizes so that they can be easily merged. Starting from those sub-regions, the similarity is computed for each pair of them to iteratively merge the most similar pairs into single regions until the whole image gets merged. At each iteration, every region which satisfies the conditions of an object (e.g., size and scale) is considered as a candidate. Naturally, sub-regions are not supposed to be similar in their content since the goal is to merge sub-regions belonging to the same object. Rather, two connected sub-regions r_i and r_j are merged based on the continuity of their spatial characteristics which is measured by the complementary similarity $S(r_i, r_j)$. For a robust similarity measurement, $S(r_i, r_j)$ consists of colour, texture and edge measurements denoted by $S_c(r_i, r_j)$, $S_h(r_i, r_j)$ and $S_e(r_i, r_j)$, respectively. The similarity measurement S_f in terms of the feature $f \in \{c, h, e\}$ is computed as the following bin-wise normalised intersection:

$$S_f(r_i, r_j) = \sum_{k=1}^{n_f} \frac{\min\left(c_{f,i}^k, c_{f,j}^k\right)}{\max\left(c_{f,i}^k, c_{f,j}^k\right)} \quad . \tag{3.1}$$

The above equation represents the normalised intersection of the histograms $c_{f,i}$ and $c_{f,j}$ extracted from the ith and j^{th} regions, respectively, where n_f denotes the histogram length. For each bin in the histogram, the intersection result lies between 0 and 1, where the absolute intersection "*numerator*" is normalised by the maximum value of the corresponding bin in both histograms "*denominator*". Figure 3.4 shows an example of histograms extracted from a query image, where the computation of each one is given blow:

Colour: In order to ensure the colour gradation between merged sub-regions, a colour-based similarity is used for this measurement. Here, the colour histogram c_c is the con-

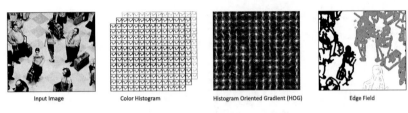

| Input Image | Color Histogram | Histogram Oriented Gradient (HOG) | Edge Field |

Figure 3.4: An example of the extracted histograms for a query image.

catenation of histograms corresponding to the three RGB channels. For each channel, the histogram is computed using 25 bins, where the length of the resulting colour histogram is $n_c = 75$. For reasonable similarity computation, colour histograms are normalised using the L_1 norm.

Texture: The second measurement ensures the texture continuity of merged regions. Given a sub-region, c_h denotes the vectorised histogram of gradient orientation features that are extracted using the open source library *VLFeat* [VF08]. Here, a region is considered as one cell, and the histogram length $n_c = 31$ corresponds to the spanning features.

Edge: Finally, objects' parts are assumed to be inside the same closed edge. Therefore, *Sobel filter* is applied to the query image in order to extract the edge map, in which each closed contour is considered as a single edge-field. The edge histogram c_e represents then the cross-frequency of the corresponding region with all edge-fields. The length of edge histogram n_e is the number of extracted edge-fields.

3.2.2   Classification

After extracting all possible candidate regions, each one is represented by its CNN-based features in order to be classified into either positive or negative. In this respect, an SVM model is priorly trained, using a manually labelled data. When all candidates are classified, negative ones are directly discarded, while positive ones are iteratively combined until forming reasonable object regions. Specifically, the most reliable candidate called "anchor" is selected among the remaining candidates at each iteration, where the reliability is measured by the classification confidence score ($\geqslant 0.3$). Afterwards, the anchor sequentially composes a combination by gathering positive candidates that sufficiently overlap ($\geqslant 30\%$) with the last combination. The step of selecting anchors is repeated until no reliable candidates left. Also, the composition step is repeated for each anchor until no overlapping candidates left.

To build the linear SVM classifier, a training data is prepared by applying the method described in 3.2.1. The positive set consists of 2000 uncut regions of the desired object, where samples are manually proofed in order not to include any excess from the surrounding. The negative set consists of 8000 samples of non-object regions, where samples in this set simply denote the non-selected regions in the positive set. For stable classification, negative samples are allowed to overtake positive areas with maximum 30% of their sizes.

3.3 Summary

Two methods dedicated to object detection are introduced in this chapter, with the aim to detect objects (e.g., people) in crowded scenes. First, a key-point-based method is presented in Section 3.1, where a pedestrian is detected with the assumption that it is described by a cluster of feature points sharing similar characteristics [Bou+16a]. Moreover, the method is extended to consider the sequence of frames as an important cue to improve the detection. Subsequently, Section 3.2 presents a more generic method which detects objects by searching for probable regions being more likely to contain the desired objects. By extracting CNN-based features from each region, a supervised learning approach is used to validate or deny the extracted candidates. The contribution of this chapter resides effectively in detecting objects under severe circumstances, notably, crowded scenes. Both methods presented in this chapter are evaluated in Section 7.1, demonstrating their strengths and weaknesses.

Chapter 4

3D Trajectory Extraction from Surveillance Videos

Extracting 3D trajectories of objects from 2D videos is problematic due to the lack of depth perception in such videos. Precisely, the metric distances, sizes and dimensions of objects are lost once they are projected from the real world onto an image plane. Figure 4.1 illustrates a concrete example in the real world of a football player passing a ball to another player, in which both of the players, the ball and the camera are located on the same longitudinal line. Consequently, the projections of the players and the ball are overlapped on the image plane, and hence human perception is needed to understand the scene.

To this end, human beings can easily understand complex scenes from 2D videos/images without the help of depth information due to their ability to learn from examples. This has inspired researchers to estimate depths in 2D videos/images by referring to depths in visually similar video/image examples [HEH08; KLK16; KLK14; SSN09; SCN08]. In this section, a combination of depth estimation and object detection is proposed to extract *3D trajectories*

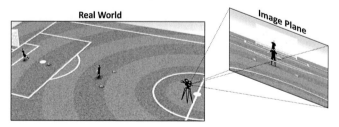

Figure 4.1: An example of information loss after projection onto the image plane.

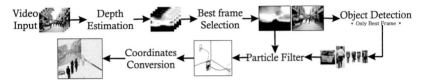

Figure 4.2: An illustration of the proposed 3D trajectory extraction based on the combination of object detection and depth estimation.

of objects from 2D stationary videos (e.g., surveillance) [Bou+15b; Bou+15a]. Here, the 3D trajectory of an object refers to its sequential positions in the 3D space over time.

Figure 4.2 illustrates the pipeline of the proposed 3D trajectory extraction method. First, depth estimation and object detection are performed for each frame of the input video [Bou+15b]. Since the accuracy of the estimated depth varies from one frame to another, a selection process of the best frame is proposed. The best frame is the one with the highest consistency score, whose depths are assumed to be convergent within the region of each object, and divergent on boundaries between object regions and the background. Afterwards, the 3D position of each object is defined in a temporal coordinates given its estimated 2D position in the image plane and its estimated depth.

Subsequently, each object in the 3D space is tracked using a particle filter, which is a time-series modelling approach approximating the non-linear probability distribution of a hidden state with random samples (particles) [Aru+02]. In this case, the hidden state denotes the object's position on the image plane, its height and its width. Finally, the sequential positions of each object are converted from the temporal coordinate system into the camera coordinate system. Each phase in the pipeline is described in the following:

4.1   Initialisation

Given an input video, the depth map of each frame is estimated using the method proposed in [KLK16] according to the reported performance comparison[1]. The method transfers depths between visually similar example images based on corresponding points with the query frame im_t at time t. The resulting output is the estimated depths of all pixels in the frame im_t, known as the *depth map* ($\mathcal{D}_t$). For object detection, the method proposed in [Fel+10] is adopted, since its generality and effectiveness have been validated in several existing studies. This method detects an object's region by considering the positions and deformations of its parts, each of which is characterised as a filter that describes the part's

---

[1]http://make3d.cs.cornell.edu/results_stateoftheart.html

shape. In a case that some objects are detected, the method's output comprises at the end bounding boxes that define each single object.

4.2 Best Frame Selection

At this stage, a video consists of sequential frames $im_{1...L}$, each of which is associated with an estimated depth map and a set of detected objects. Here, the best frame is selected assuming that its depth map has the smoothest continuity of depth in the regions defined by edges, and the largest difference in depths between regions separated by edges. In this endeavour, a *Depth Consistency Score* (S) is computed for all frames of the video sequence. Thus, C_t is the edge map at time t, which is obtained by applying a Canny edge detector to im_t.

Based on the assumption that depths in $\mathcal{D}_t$ are spatially continuous, except on the edges in C_t, the depth consistency score of im_t $(S(im_t))$ is computed as follows:

$$S(im_t) = \underbrace{\frac{S_1(im_t)}{\sum_{l=1}^{L} S_1(im_l)}}_{a} + \underbrace{\frac{\sum_{l=1}^{L} S_2(im_l)}{S_2(im_t)}}_{b} \quad , \tag{4.1}$$

where L denotes the number of frames in the video. Equation 4.1 is computed as the summation of two terms, where Equation 4.1(a) controls the spatial continuity of depths in non-edge regions and Equation 4.1(b) controls the depth discontinuity in edge regions. For Equation 4.1(a), $S_1(im_t)$ is computed as follows:

$$S_1(im_t) = \frac{1}{\sum_{i=1}^{W}\sum_{j=1}^{H} C_t(i,j)} \sum_{i=1}^{W} \sum_{j=1}^{H} C_t(i,j) \times V_t(i,j) \quad , \tag{4.2}$$

where $C_t(i,j)$ is a binary value that is returned as 1 if the pixel at the position (i,j) is observed as a non-edge, otherwise $C_t(i,j) = 0$. W and H denote the width and height of im_t, respectively. $V_t(i,j)$ represents the continuity of depths at (i,j) given by the following difference:

$$V_t(i,j) = \max_{\substack{i-1 \leq m,m' \leq i+1 \\ j-1 \leq n,n' \leq j+1}} |\mathcal{D}_t(m,n) - \mathcal{D}_t(m',n')| \quad . \tag{4.3}$$

Equation 4.3 computes the maximum depth difference within the 3-by-3 region, whose centre is (i,j). Since Equation 4.2 does not consider edge regions, $S_1(im_t)$ represents the mean of V_t in non-edge pixels. In contrast, $S_2(im_t)$ in Equation 4.1(b) is the mean of V_t in edge pixels computed on the inverse edge map C'_t, where $C'_t(i,j) = 1$ if the pixel at (i,j) is regarded as an edge, otherwise $C'_t(i,j) = 0$. S_2 is computed then as follows:

$$S_2(im_t) = \frac{1}{\sum_{i=1}^{W}\sum_{j=1}^{H}C'_t(i,j)}\sum_{i=1}^{W}\sum_{j=1}^{H}C'_t(i,j) \times V_t(i,j) \quad . \tag{4.4}$$

Eventually, the best frame is chosen to be the one with the highest $S(.)$ among all frames in the video. Moreover, the depth of each detected object in the best frame is considered as the mean of the depth values inside its bounding box, so that its 3D position can be obtained.

4.3   Particle Filter

For any detected object Δ_0 in the best frame im_0 of the video, a forward and backwards tracking processes are performed [Bou+15a]. In this respect, the proposed method makes use of an independent particle filter, which estimates the probability distribution of all hypotheses of the object's positions. It is important to note that there is no technical difference between forward and backwards tracking. Therefore, only forward tracking is described in this section, with backwards tracking simply being its inverse. Let $\mathbf{q}_0 = (x_0, y_0, w_0, h_0, Z'_0)$ be the initial state denoting the 3D position of any target object Δ_0 in a temporal coordinates. Here, 'the temporality' is due to the non-homogeneity of the coordinate system, where a conversion to 3D coordinates is needed. More specifically, (x, y) represents the top-left position of the object's bounding box, which returned by the object detector. This box is characterised with a width w and height h on the image plane, where its visual appearance for Δ_0 is indicated by ROI_0. Moreover, Z'_0 is the estimated depth, denoting the distance between the object and the camera in the real world. Considering that the N particles initially indicate the same state $\mathbf{q}_0$, the object's 3D position $\mathbf{q}_t = (x_t, y_t, w_t, h_t, Z'_t)$ is estimated at each time t.

Essentially, the particle filter approximates the posterior probability density of a hidden state using a set of particles, which are randomly sampled and then weighted for a given sequence of observations. In this work, $\mathbf{q}_t$ is considered a hidden state at time t and $ROI_{0:t} = (ROI_0, \cdots, ROI_t)$ is the sequence of the visual appearances of the object's bounding box from the best frame to the tth one. The posterior probability distribution is approximated as follows:

$$p(\mathbf{q}_t|ROI_{0:t}) \approx \sum_{i=1}^{N}\omega_t^i\,\delta(\mathbf{q}_t - \mathbf{q}_t^i) \quad , \tag{4.5}$$

where $\delta(.)$ is the Dirac delta function. The ith particle is represented by the pair $\{\mathbf{q}_t^i, \omega_t^i\}$, where $\mathbf{q}_t^i$ denotes the ith random sample for $\mathbf{q}_t$, and ω_t^i is the weight representing the probability of

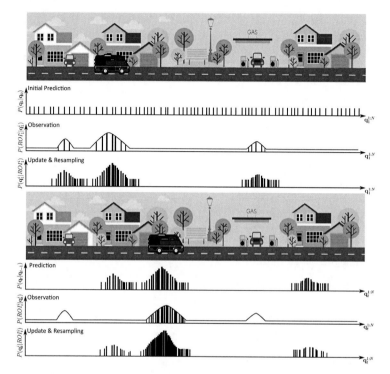

Figure 4.3: An overview of the tracking process using particle filter.

$\mathbf{q}_t^i$ ($\sum_{i=1}^{N} \omega_t^i \simeq 1$). The estimation of the object's 3D position for the tth frame is regarded as $\mathbf{q}_t^i$ with the highest probability, and as $\mathbf{q}_t$ in the subsequent process. At every frame, $p(\mathbf{q}_t|ROI_{0:t})$ is approximated according to the particle filtering framework [Aru+02], by iterating the three processes illustrated in Figure 4.3:

1. Prediction: Given the probability distribution $\mathbf{q}_{t-1}$ at $t-1$, N particles are sampled in order to estimate $\mathbf{q}_t$ for the tth frame from the transition (prior) distribution $p(\mathbf{q}_t|\mathbf{q}_{t-1})$. In Section 4.3.1, the transition distribution is modelled based on the velocity of Δ.

2. Update: For each sample $\mathbf{q}_t^i$, the weight ω_t^i is determined by computing the probability $p(ROI_t^i|\mathbf{q}_t^i)$, which represents the extent of similarity between the corresponding bounding box to $\mathbf{q}_t^i$ (ROI_t^i) and the validated appearance of the object (ROI_0). Consequently, the posterior distribution in Equation 4.5 is updated after the formulation of each particle $\{\mathbf{q}_t^i, \omega_t^i\}$. Assuming that ROI_0 correctly defines Δ, $p(ROI_t^i | \mathbf{q}_t^i)$ is computed by extracting and matching correspondence points between ROI_t^i and ROI_0. This is discussed in greater detail in Section 4.3.2.

3. Resampling: Due to the high number of sampled particles, it is natural for their weights to vary and several of them to have a negligible value. Therefore, this process resamples N particles based on the distribution obtained in the update process, where particles with lower weights are reassigned to those with higher weights [Aru+02]. In this work, all particles are resampled to the one with the highest weight, whose corresponding $\mathbf{q}_t^*$ is the estimated object's 3D position. Therefore, the same weight $(1/N)$ is uniformly assigned to each particle. The reason for resampling to one particle is to consistently sample N particles at each time t, during which the potential loss of other high weighted particles is compensated in the prediction process.

4.3.1   Transition Distribution

The transition distribution $p(\mathbf{q}_t | \mathbf{q}_{t-1})$ is modelled based on the first-order AutoRegressive (AR) process. Let $v_t = [v^x{}_t, v^y{}_t, v^z{}_t]^\mathsf{T}$ be the displacement (velocity) of Δ between the $(t-1)^{th}$ and t^{th} frames on the x, y and z axes. Due to the unavailability of the velocity in the first frame, $v^x{}_0$, $v^y{}_0$ and $v^z{}_0$ are manually initialised, where $v^x{}_0 = W/6$ and $v^y{}_0 = H/6$. Regarding the velocity on the z axis that is measured in metric unit, $v^z{}_0 = 2 \times 10^2$mm for slow objects such as pedestrians, and $v^z{}_0 = 2 \times 10^4$mm for fast objects like cars. For subsequent frames, the velocity is updated to $v_t = v_{t-1} - v_{t-2}$. Given the state of Δ at $t-1$ ($\mathbf{q}_{t-1} = (x_{t-1}, y_{t-1}, w_{t-1}, h_{t-1}, Z'_{t-1})$) and its current velocity v_t, N particles ($\{\mathbf{q}_t^i\}_{i=1}^N$) from $p(\mathbf{q}_t | \mathbf{q}_{t-1})$ are sampled for the tth frame. For an accurate sampling, the N particles must cover all possible regions that are more likely to contain the object. However, this is extremely time consuming for a random sampling process, where a large number of particles is required. Therefore, the N particles are strategically sampled in order to capture the overall characteristic of $p(\mathbf{q}_t | \mathbf{q}_{t-1})$.

To accomplish this, N is equally divided over the three axes, where the same number of particles is sampled on each axis by fulfilling $N = a^x \cdot a^y \cdot a^z + r$. Here, a^x, a^y and a^z are discrete values that represent the number of sampled particles on x, y and z axes, respectively, where N is the combination of the three of them. Furthermore, the discrete value on each axis in supposed to be proportional to the velocity on the same axis to ensure a fair division, where $|v^x/a^x| \approx |v^y/a^y| \approx |v^z/10a^z|$. Assuming that objects maintain or change their velocity smoothly on each axis, the particles of the corresponding axis are densely sampled around two positions: (1) the one that is predicted based on the position at $t-1$ and the velocity at t,

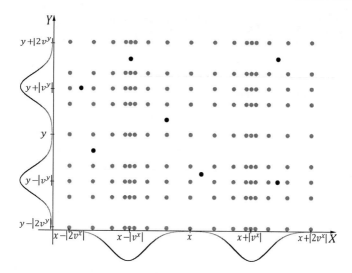

Figure 4.4: A 2D view of N selected samples.

and (2) the reverse of the predicted one (e.g., $x_{t-1} \pm v^x{}_t$ for the x axis). Although it is axiomatic that the object is less likely to occur around the reverse predicted position, this hypothesis is considered in this work with the aim to compensate any potential inaccurate tracking in the previous frames ($< t$). This is especially adopted because all particles are resampled to only one particle at the end of each tracking iteration. The sampling of a known number of particles (a^x, a^y or a^z) is considered a mixture distribution, as shown in Figure 4.4, where the remaining r particles are randomly sampled to obtain N particles. Figure 4.4 illustrates a 2D view of N samples, where the bright points represent particles that are systematically sampled by combining a^x, a^y and a^z, and the dark points are randomly sampled (r). Finally, h^i_t and w^i_t of $\mathbf{q}^i_t$ are determined by linearly scaling h_0 and w_0 of $\mathbf{q}_0$ based on the inverse ratio of Z'^i_t to Z'_0 (i.e., $h^i_t = h_0 \times Z'_0/Z'^i_t$ and $w^i_t = w_0 \times Z'_0/Z'^i_t$).

4.3.2 Weight Computation

In order to form the particle $\{\mathbf{q}^i_t, \omega^i_t\}$, the weight ω^i_t is computed as the similarity between the visual appearance ROI^i_t and that of the reference region ROI_0 [Bou+15b]. However, the appearance of any object evolves over time in an image sequence due to its movements, shape deformation, illumination change, etc. To overcome this and to robustly align sequential bounding boxes defining Δ in the sequence, the SIFT flow is used to produce the dense,

$$f_0(\mathbf{q}_0) \quad\quad f_t(\mathbf{q}_t^1) \quad f_t(\mathbf{q}_t^2) \quad f_t(\mathbf{q}_t^3) \quad\quad f_t(\mathbf{q}_t^N)$$

Figure 4.5: An illustration of the SIFT flow matching.

pixel-to-pixel correspondence between ROI_t^i and ROI_0 [LYT11], by matching SIFT descriptors instead of raw pixels. The idea is to extract the SIFT descriptor at each pixel in ROI_0 in order to characterise the local image structure and encode the contextual information. Subsequently, the discrete discontinuity preserving flow estimation algorithm is used to match the SIFT descriptors with ROI_t^i.

Figure 4.5 illustrates the process of matching ROI_0 with the generated bounding boxes $ROI_t^{1:N}$ using the SIFT flow, where the movement of Δ on the z axis controls the size of its bounding box by making it larger or smaller. As displayed in Figure 4.5, the bounding box defined by $\mathbf{q}_t^i$ is first resized to the same size as the one defined by $\mathbf{q}_0$. Afterwards, the matching score of ROI_t^i with ROI_0 is obtained by the energy function $E(ROI_t^i, ROI_0)$, which represents a pixel displacement field. In Figure 4.5, the pixels (o) in ROI_0 correspond to the pixels (+) in ROI_t^i, where ROI_t^3 is judged as the most similar to ROI_0 because of the smallest energy. This is based on the sum of the line lengths between os and +s with the same colours. Using such an energy, the similarity between ROI_t^i and ROI_0 is measured as $1/E(ROI_t^i, ROI_0)$, and used as a weight ω_t^i for the ith particle.

After weighting all the particles, the state of the one with the maximum weight $(\mathbf{q}_t^*)$ is considered the object's 3D position $\mathbf{q}_t$ for the tth frame. Moreover, since the appearance of Δ may significantly change according to the development of the video, ROI_0 is updated so that it adaptively follows the latest appearance of the object. Thus, a parameter ψ_t is introduced $(\psi_t = \omega_t / \max\{\omega_l\}_{l=1}^t)$ to normalise ω_t using the maximum weight for all previously computed weights. ROI_0 is then updated with ROI_t if ψ_t is greater than or equal to a determined threshold, assuming that a high similarity between ROI_0 and ROI_t indicates that $\mathbf{q}_t$ reliably defines the object. Conversely, a low similarity between ROI_0 and ROI_t would indicate that the estimated $\mathbf{q}_t$ is not as reliable. Consequently, another threshold is determined, with

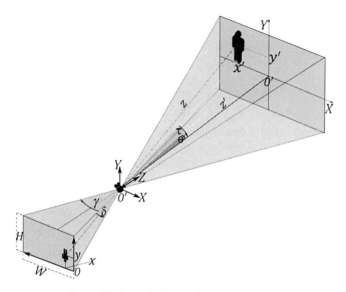

Figure 4.6: A standard optical geometry system.

which ψ is compared. If ψ is less than the new new threshold, then $\mathbf{q}_t$ is considered unreliable and the displacement (v^x_t, v^y_t, v^z_t) is equal to $(2 \times v^x_{t-1}, 2 \times v^y_{t-1}, 2 \times v^z_{t-1})$. The reason for this is to ensure that an unreliable estimation of $\mathbf{q}_t$ is not used to compute the displacement. Thus the 3D position for the $(t+1)^{th}$ is searched in a larger region.

4.4 Coordinate Conversion

For each state estimation $\mathbf{q}_t$ at time t, x and y denote the position (in pixel unit) of the object on the image plane (presented on the left side in Figure 4.6), and Z' is the distance between Δ and the camera in metric unit (depicted in the right side of Figure 4.6) [Bou+15a]. To accomplish this, a conversion process is performed based on the laws of optical geometry [Kat02], so that the state clearly indicates the object's position in a uniform coordinate system. Accordingly, the estimated x, y, Z' are converted into X, Y, Z in the camera coordinate (real world), where the origin is at the centre of the camera, as illustrated in Figure 4.6.

Since cameras provide images with different aspect ratios, default horizontal and vertical angle of views, γ' and δ' are assumed to be equal to 60° and 45°, respectively, with an aspect ratio of (3:4). On this basis, the angle of views γ and δ of the considered video can be computed as follows:

$$[\gamma,\delta] = \begin{cases} \gamma', & \delta' & \text{if } \frac{W}{H} \simeq \frac{4}{3} \\ \gamma', & 2\arctan\left(\frac{4\,h\,\tan(\frac{\delta'}{2})}{3\,W}\right) & \text{if } \frac{W}{H} > \frac{4}{3} \\ 2\arctan\left(\frac{3\,W\,\tan(\frac{\gamma'}{2})}{4\,H}\right), & \delta' & \text{if } \frac{W}{H} < \frac{4}{3} \end{cases}, \tag{4.6}$$

where the maximum horizontal and vertical angles of view for a normal camera are assumed not to exceed γ' and δ', respectively, and vary according to the aspect ratio. As illustrated in Figure 4.6, τ is formed by the axis OZ' and the vector OX, while θ is formed by the axis OZ' and the vector OX. Given γ and δ, the angles τ and θ are computed:

$$\begin{cases} \tau = \arctan(\frac{2(x-\frac{W}{2})\tan(\frac{\gamma}{2})}{W}) \\ \theta = \arctan(\frac{2(y-\frac{H}{2})\tan(\frac{\delta}{2})}{H}) \end{cases}. \tag{4.7}$$

Thus, the object's 3D position (X,Y,Z) in the real world can be calculated as $X = \sin(\tau)Z'$, $Y = \sin(\theta)Z'$ and $Z = \cos(\tau)\cos(\theta)Z'$.

4.5   Summary

This chapter introduced a method to extract the 3D trajectory of an individual object by combining object detection and depth estimation [Bou+15b; Bou+15a]. The main idea is to find the best frame, in which estimated depths using [KLK16] are more likely to be consistent. This process is addressed to ensure the reliability of the estimated depths of the objects for tracking purposes. Starting from the best frame, the detected object is tracked forward and backward on the image plane using a particle filter with the help of SIFT matching. The change in the size of object's bounding box is considered to be a cue that indicates the object's movements on the longitudinal axis. At the end of each filtering iteration, the obtained coordinate is converted from the image plane into the real world. The main contribution of this chapter is the extraction of 3D trajectories using 2D videos. In Section 7.2.1, a detailed experiment of the extraction of 3D trajectories is presented along with the result.

Chapter 5

3D Trajectory Extraction from Moving Cameras

Extracting 3D trajectories of objects from 2D uncalibrated moving videos is more complicated and cannot be achieved using the method described in Chapter4, which tracks objects on the image plane, then converts the obtained position into the real world coordinate system. This complication is due to the identicalness of the real world coordinate system with the camera coordinate system. However, for cases including moving cameras, the camera coordinate system is different from the real world one, as illustrated in Figure 5.1. For this reason, the proposed solution is to directly track both the objects and the camera in the real world [BSG17a]. In such a case, the position's hypotheses are generated in the real world. Afterwards, each hypothesis is evaluated based on its projection onto the image plane w.r.t the development of the camera coordinate system.

To tackle this issue, it is proposed in this chapter to first estimate the focal length of the camera in order to connect the image plane with the camera coordinate system. The estimated focal length is used to estimate the depths of detected objects in the initial frame and to afterwards project objects' hypotheses from the real world onto the image plane. Subsequently, RJ-MCMC particle filtering is employed to simultaneously estimate the 3D positions of the camera and multiple objects Δ_t at each time t w.r.t the camera Φ_t. Specifically, the particle filter is used to estimate the probability distribution of all hypothesis, each of which represents the 3D positions of the camera and objects. Figure 5.2 illustrates the diagram of the adopted RJ-MCMC particle filter with the configuration Θ_t, which contains the camera's position Φ_t and the set of objects' positions Δ_t at each time $t > 0$. In the remaining of this chapter, Δ^i is used to interchangeably indicate the ith object or its state (3D position) as far as it is clear from the context. Each particle (proposal) $(1 \le j \le N)$ at time t transfers (jumps from) the configuration Θ_t^j to Θ_t^{j+1}, by generating either 'camera move', 'object move',

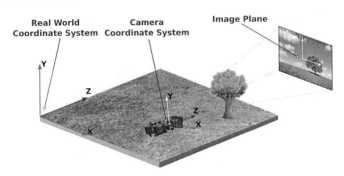

Figure 5.1: An overview of the difference between world coordinate system, camera coordinate system and image plane.

'object birth' or 'object death'. Thus, the jump is evaluated given the observation (visual characteristics) Ψ_t and the previous configuration Θ_{t-1}, where the new proposal $j+1$ is accepted only if it is better than the previous one (j).

The problem of extracting the 3D trajectories of objects is formulated as obtaining the Maximum A Posteriori (MAP) estimation. To this end, the posterior distribution $P(\Theta_t|\Psi_t)$ is determined over the current joint configuration of the camera Φ_t at t and the set of objects, given all observations $\Psi_{0,..,t} = \Psi_1, ... \Psi_t$. The MAP solution of the posterior distribution can be formulated as follows:

$$P(\Theta_t|\Psi_{0,..,t}) \propto \underbrace{P(\Psi_t|\Theta_t)}_{a} \int \underbrace{P(\Theta_t|\Theta_{t-1})}_{b} \underbrace{P(\Theta_{t-1}|\Psi_{0,..,t-1})}_{c} d\Theta_{t-1} \quad . \tag{5.1}$$

Equation 5.1 keeps the mathematical generality described in [Aru+02], where Equation5.1(a) is the likelihood part that expresses the measurement model of the configuration Θ_t given the observation Ψ_t. The observation model controls the appearance of the projection of a given object in the image plane based on its state and that of the camera. This is performed using key-point matching [VF08]. Additionally, this model controls the pixel displacement caused by the camera movements [BSG17b]. Equation5.1(b) represents the motion model which controls the smoothness of the movement of both the camera and the objects as well as their interactions. More specifically, the motion model restricts the proposed movements of the objects at t (Θ_t) on the basis of their previous movements at $t-1$ (Θ_{t-1}), and thus narrowing the search space for the best configuration. Finally, Equation 5.1(c) represents the posterior probability at time $t-1$. The centre of the real world coordinate system is initialised as the position of the camera at $t=0$. Moreover, the positions

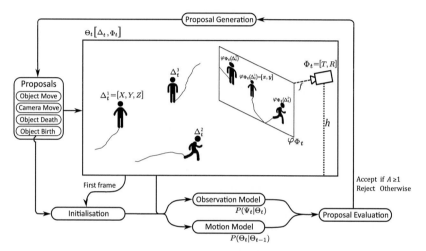

Figure 5.2: A general overview of the proposed system. First, the detected objects are projected into the real world coordinate system. After that, proposals for N particles are repeatedly generated and evaluated by employing both the observation model $P(\Psi_t|\Theta_t)$ and the motion model $P(\Theta_t|\Theta_{t-1})$. Once a new object enters into the scene, its information is captured and passed by the object detection process.

of the existing objects Δ_0 are computed w.r.t Φ_0 based on two factors: (1) their bounding boxes given by the object detector and (2) their priorly computed depths (Section 5.2). Initially, the N particles are considered to indicate the same configuration $\Theta_0^{1:N}$ and the same posterior probability $(1/N)$ is uniformly assigned to each particle. In summary, the detailed steps of the RJ-MCMC particle filtering for simultaneously tracking several objects and the camera are given in the following algorithm:

Algorithm 2: Detailed steps of the adopted RJ-MCMC particle filtering

At each time step t, the configuration state is represented by a set of samples $\{\Theta_{t-1}^j\}_{j=1}^N$.

1   Initialisation of the RJ-MCMC sampler:

- The sample Θ_{t-1}^* that maximise the MAP solution is selected.

- The camera Φ_{t-1}^* and all objects Δ_{t-1}^* in the corresponding configuration Θ_{t-1}^* are moved based on their motion model (Section 5.4). The result is the initial configuration Θ_t^j in the current frame t.

- The observation likelihood of Θ_t^j is evaluated (Section 5.3).

2   RJ-MCMC sampling steps with $(B + MN)$ iterations, where B is the number of discarded samples in order to burn-in the sampler. M is the thinning interval which is used to avoid correlation among samples:

- From the previous configuration Θ_t^j, either the camera or a random object is picked to sample a new configuration Θ_t^{j+1} based on randomly selected jumps (Section 5.5).

- The acceptance ratio A is computed (Equation 5.18).

- If $(A \geq 1)$, then the new sample is accepted Θ_t^{j+1}, rejected otherwise $(\Theta_t^{j+1} = \Theta_t^j)$.

3   After the initial B burn-in iterations, every M^{th} is stored in order to approximate the current posterior.

In the above algorithm, B is the number of samples used to stabilise (burn-in) the system, where they are not considered for subsequent computation. Also, a sample is kept only after M interval from the last kept one. This is used to avoid correlation between samples. For a better interpretation, Fig 5.3 summarises the steps described in Algorithm 2, illustrating an example of one iteration of estimating the posterior distribution. Below, detailed explanations about focal length estimation, object's depth estimation, observation model, motion model and sampling process are given:

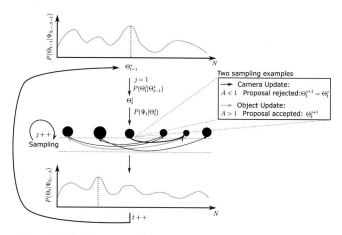

Figure 5.3: An illustration of the adopted RJ-MCMC particle filtering.

5.1 Focal Length Estimation

The focal length (physical length of the lens) is an important key to capture sensible images, where it is proportional to the size of a 2D object projection. Moreover, it has an inverse relationship with the largeness of Field-Of-View (FOV). In practice, the focal length is tuned based on the desired view to be captured and the distance to the target objects. Particularly, distant objects (e.g., natural view) require a large focal length, while close ones (e.g., indoor) need a shorter focal length. Furthermore, the blurry intensity of the background and the number of acquired objects are highly dependent on the focal length. Hence, these characteristics can be considered as good clues to inversely estimate the focal length [BSG17a]. However, they do not express concrete values and are not straightly connected to the focal length value. In addition to the focal length, some of these characteristics (e.g., the largeness of FOV and the number of objects) are controlled by the size of the Charge-Coupled Device (CCD). In the subsequent processes, the focal length is expressed in pixel unit, which is computed given the physical length of the lens, the size of the CCD sensor and the width of the image. Since the size of the image is ever available and it varies in a wide range, it is proposed to estimate the ratio $l = \frac{f_{mm}}{\eta}$, where f_{mm} denotes the physical length of the lens, and η denotes the width of the CCD sensor. Thus, the focal length becomes $f = W \times l$, where W is the width of the image.

Given a query image, the corresponding l is estimated by searching for the ls of images that have similar characteristics. Accordingly, the training dataset consists of 75000 images

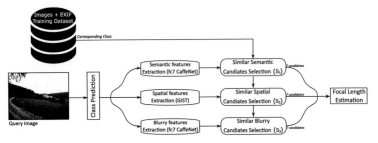

Figure 5.4: An overview of the focal length estimation method.

correlated with Exchangeable Image File Format (EXIF) files, which is collected from *Mir-flickr*[1] [HTL10]. Those images were taken from different cameras covering a large range of focal lengths in a variety of semantic classes. With this, each training image is associated with the corresponding scene and annotated with its focal lengths in advance.

Figure 5.4 presents an overview of estimating l from similar examples, where the query image is first classified using multi-class SVM based on the features of semantic content that are extracted from the **fc7** layer of BVLC-CaffeNet [2] using Caffe framework [Jia+14]. Caffe is a deep convolutional neural network framework allowing to extract a high-dimensional (4096-dimensions) feature which describes the semantic content of a given image. In observance of the class of the query image, only training images belonging to the same class are considered, from which a set (S_1) of 100 candidates is selected. This is achieved by using GIST descriptors [OT01], which permit to retrieve images with similar spatial characteristics. Next, the extracted features from BVLC-CaffeNet are used in order to select a new set (S_2) of 20 candidates from S_1, so that the new set contains only similar semantic images. Then, a new set (S_3) of seven image candidates is selected from S_2, where S_3 should contain similar images with close blurry degree [LLJ08] as the query image. Finally, seven candidates with the highest similarities are selected from every set, where l is estimated by minimising the following objective function $E(l)$:

$$E(l) = a.E_1(l, \hat{l}_{1:7}^1) + b.E_2(l, \hat{l}_{1:7}^2) + c.E_3(l, \hat{l}_{1:7}^3) \quad,$$
$$\text{where } E_j = \sum_{i=1}^{7} w_i^j (|l - \hat{l}_i^j|) \quad. \tag{5.2}$$

Here, $E(l)$ is defined as the linear combination of three terms E_1, E_2 and E_3 denoting spatial similarity, semantic similarity and blurry similarity, respectively. a, b and c are given parameters, which are priorly calculated (detailed in Section 7.3.1). For every E_j, w_i

---

[1]http://press.liacs.nl/mirflickr/

[2]https://github.com/BVLC/caffe/tree/master/models/bvlc_reference_caffenet

represents the similarity between the query image and the ith candidate image, which is given by the corresponding similarity measurement. Moreover, $\hat{l}_i$ is the ratio of focal length (in millimetre) to the CCD width of the ith image candidate.

5.2 Object's Depth Estimation

In the first frame, every object is expressed by a bounding box and an associated object category, which are both given by the object detector. Thus, objects are defined only on the image plane and cannot be localised in the real world due to the lack of depth information. Basically, the size of the detected bounding box is subject to the real size of the corresponding object and its distance from the camera (depth). It is obvious that close and bigger objects in the real world occupy bigger space on the image plane. Consequently, the object's depth can be computed in function of the focal length, the size of the object in the real world and the size of its projection on the image plane using the pinhole camera geometry [HZ04]. Since only the sizes of objects in the real world are missing, it is proposed to estimate the height and width of every object in the scene [BSG17a]. This ensures a small error drift compared to direct depth estimation, with the assumption that objects of the same category have sizes in a specific range. Therefore, the size of a given object in the real world is simply computed as the mean of the real-world sizes of its most similar candidates in the training dataset.

For this issue, a training dataset is used, which consists of bounding boxes of five classes of objects (Person, Car, Track, Cyclist and Motorbike), each bounding box is associated with the corresponding size in the real world. The size of an object region can be then estimated by considering the sizes of selected candidates from the same class. The selection of candidates is performed based on their appearance similarities to the query image in term of GIST [OT01] descriptors. Then the mean size of all candidates is assigned to the query object.

5.3 Observation Model

In order to find the best configuration for the input data, a configuration hypothesis is evaluated by measuring the matching between its projection and the available evidence w.r.t the current camera pose. The observation model is then the product of all measurements and can be represented as follows:

$$P(\Psi_t|\Theta_t) = P(\Psi t|\Phi_t) \prod_t P(\Psi_t|\varphi_{\Phi_t}(\Delta_t^i)) \quad . \tag{5.3}$$

In the above equation, $P(\Psi_t|\Phi_t)$ measures the camera movement from $t-1$ to t considering the flow similarity. $P(\Psi_t | \varphi_{\Phi_t}(\Delta_t^i))$ measures the hypothesis of birth (entering the scene), death (leaving the scene) or movement of the tth object Δ_t^i in Δ_t. Here, the hypothesis of an object's birth is measured by the object detector. The hypothesis of the death or movement of an object is measured based on a matching similarity between the projection of $\Delta_t^{i(j)}$ onto the image plane at t w.r.t camera parameters Φ_t and its last valid appearance ROI_0^t. In the following, the observation likelihood of the camera and an object i from Δ are given in the following:

5.3.1 Camera Observation

In the real world, the camera moves with six degrees of freedom divided equally to rotational and transnational movements. This makes the estimation of its pose difficult, especially because only few information can be retrieved (i.e., correspondence of 2D pixels between sequential images) from monocular videos that lack metric information. Additionally, visual odometry estimation is very sensitive to rotational drifts, regardless of its smallness, where its accumulation causes an enormous change in the estimated trajectory of the camera over time. For this reason, it is proposed to use the available information to estimate the rotation (R_t) and translation $(\hat{T}_t)$ between each two consecutive frames im_{t-1} and im_t, where the translation is "*up to scale*" [BSG17b]. In other words, the estimated $(\hat{T}_t)$ expresses only the proportion of movements along each axis. More precisely, (R_t) and $(\hat{T}_t)$ are estimated by decomposing the essential matrix $\mathcal{E}$, which is computed as: $\mathcal{E} = \mathcal{K}^\mathsf{T}.\mathcal{F}.\mathcal{K}$ [HZ04]. Here, $\mathcal{F}$ and $\mathcal{K}$ represent the fundamental matrix between im_{t-1} and im_t and the calibration matrix, respectively. The fundamental matrix describes the geometric relationship between two images of the same scene by relating corresponding points between them. For this, two sets of SIFT key-points q_{t-1} and q_t are detected and matched between im_{t-1} and im_t using [LYT11], where each point q_{t-1}^i corresponds to q_t^i. In order to robustly determinate $\mathcal{F}$ from the q_{t-1} and q_t, RANSAC is used to select the best pair of sets $\hat{q}_{t-1}^*$ and $\hat{q}_t^*$ (consisting of 8 matched points). The process performs N iterations until a sufficient number of matched points is by minimising the following cost function:

$$\left(\hat{q}_{t-1}^*, \hat{q}_t^*, \mathcal{F}_t^* \right) = \underset{\substack{\hat{q}_{t-1}^j \subseteq q_{t-1} \\ \hat{q}_t^j \subseteq q_t}}{\operatorname{argmin}} \left(\frac{1}{|q_t|} \sum_{i=1}^{|q_t|} d(q_{t-1}^i, q_t^i; \mathcal{F}_t^j) \right) \quad , \tag{5.4}$$

where $\mathcal{F}_t^j$ is the fundamental matrix calculated from the two sets $\hat{q}_{t-1}^j$ and $\hat{q}_t^j$ using eight-point algorithm [HZ04], where at each iteration j, $\hat{q}_{t-1}^j$ and $\hat{q}_t^j$ are randomly selected from q_{t-1} and q_t, respectively. $d(.,.;.)$ is the Sampson distance [HZ04] computed for each pair (q_{t-1}^i, q_t^i).

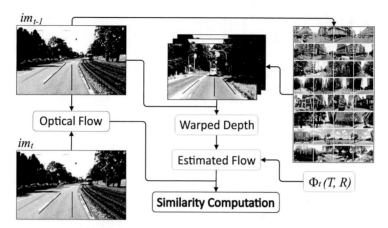

Figure 5.5: An illustration of the observation of camera odometry following the steps: 1) Computing the pixel displacement between (im_{t-1} and im_t. 2) Retrieving the 10 most similar images to im_{t-1}. 3) Matching the segments between im_{t-1} and its candidates. 4) Warping the depths of im_{t-1}'s segments. 5) Estimating the pixel displacement, given a hypothesis of camera parameters. 6) Computing the similarity.

Although the camera is supposed to move freely, it can capture stationary points from static planar surfaces (mainly the ground plane). Therefore, this characterisation is used to correct the scale drift of the priorly estimated translation ($\hat{T}_t$). Figure 5.5 illustrates the process of validating a hypothesis of correcting the scale drift based on the similarity between the two sets of key-points (Γ) and (Γ'_{Φ_t}), both of which denote 2D positions in im_t. (Γ) is obtained by tracking the initial key-points (Γ^+) from im_{t-1} to im_t. Given the estimated depth of each pixel in (Γ^+), (Γ'_{Φ_t}) is obtained by projecting (Γ^+) from im_{t-1} into the real world w.r.t Φ_{t-1} and re-projecting the output onto im_t w.r.t Φ_t^j. The camera observation is then given by the following similarity:

$$P(\Psi_t|\Phi_t) = \frac{1}{L} \sum_{j=1}^{L} \left(\frac{1}{\sqrt{\varrho\left(\Gamma^j, \Gamma'^j_{\Phi_t}\right) + 1}} \right) \quad , \tag{5.5}$$

where $\varrho(.,.)$ is the difference of pixel displacement between (Γ) and (Γ'_{Φ_t}) for the jth pixel and L denotes the number of matched pixels.

Since the availability of geometrical features is not ensured in all videos, (Γ^+) is determined as a set of pixels, whose 3D projections can comprise line segments among all pixels in im_t. Unlike classical depth estimation methods [KLK16; SSN09], which estimate the whole depth map, only supposed line segments are considered in this work, assuming that a segment extracted from a planar surface ensures the depth convergence of adjacent pixels. The reason is that the projection of key-points from the image plane into a real world differs from the projection of geometrical shapes. Precisely, a key-point has a size neither on image plane nor in a real world coordinate. First, candidates with similar semantic contents as im_{t-1} are retrieved from a training dataset that is formerly prepared. Each entity in the dataset consists of an RGB image, Gist descriptors, a depth map and a segment map, where the segments are extracted based on the homogeneous divergence of the 3D points projected into the real world. Here, only orthogonal and perpendicular segments w.r.t the optical axis are conserved. Subsequently, the method proposed by Karsch *et al.* [KLK16] is adopted to estimate the depths of segments given the depths of similar segments on the candidate images. Considering one segment in a given image candidate, every pixel is independently matched with its corresponding in im_{t-1} using [LYT11]. Afterwards, only the segment with the high matched pixels and the low disparity is selected. The remaining pixels are assigned to their corresponding ones based on the potentiality of the pixels that are priorly matched. After assigning im_{t-1}'s pixels to their counterparts in the candidate images, the minimisation function presented in [KLK16] is employed to estimate the depths of pixels that correspond to (Γ^+) in the query image. Since the pixel correspondence between im_{t-1} and im_t is already performed in the estimation of the fundamental matrix, (Γ^+) is updated as its intersection with q_{t-1} $(\Gamma^+ = \Gamma^+ \bigcup q_{t-1})$, where the corresponding pixels in q_t represent (Γ). However, if the output of the intersection is not sufficient, the initial (Γ^+) is tracked using Kanade-Lucas-Tomasi (KLT) [TK91].

In a case where the height and the relative position of segments on known planar surfaces contradict to the assumed parameters (due to wrong estimated focal length or assumed optical centre), both the translation and rotation are rectified. For example, if the projection of segments falls on lower a level than the assumed camera height, the translation on X and Y axes and also the pitch and the yaw angles are rectified by the same proportion of the height difference (between the assumed and the computed ones).

5.3.2   Object Observation

For simplicity, only movements on X and Z axes are considered, which means that all objects are assumed to be located on the ground plane as well as the camera w.r.t its height $\mho$. However, an object moves freely and independently from the camera and can enter into the scene at any moment. Therefore, an object is controlled by a birth measurement for its first appearance and by a movement measurement, subsequently [BSG17a].

Unlike [CPS13] that applies many detectors for every frame, only one detector is applied in this work. Thus the input data (initial observation) is obtained using the method proposed by Felzenszwalb *et al.* [Fel+10]. This method is used only in the first frame or in a small region for further frames when a new object's proposal is generated. The purpose is to make the system run faster even with a high number of particles (hypothesis). Given the jth proposal that updates the position of Δ^i at time t, a similarity is measured between ROI_0^i and $ROI_t^{i(j)}$, which denote the last valid appearance of Δ^i and the projection of the proposal from the 3D space into im_t w.r.t Φ_t at $t > t_0$ ($\varphi_{\Phi_t}(\Delta_t^{i(j)})$), respectively. For this, the extracted keypoints from ROI_0^i and $ROI_t^{i(j)}$ are matched using VLFeat [VF08] that can achieve fast and accurate point matching between two images, where these keypoints are extracted based on SIFT features [Low99]. In order to reduce the computational time of Equation 5.6 for all particles, keypoints are not extracted from each $ROI_t^{i(j)}$, but from the entire frame im_t. The keypoints are used in common to compute the similarity of all objects at time t. Specifically, only keypoints which are located inside $ROI_t^{i(j)}$ are considered, where if $ROI_t^{i(j)}$ does not fit completely in im_t, except the fitted part of $ROI_t^{i(j)}$ is matched with its corresponding one from ROI_0^i. The similarity $S_t^{\Delta^i}$ between ROI_0^i and $ROI_t^{i(j)}$ which represents the observation likelihood of Δ^i at each time t can be written as follows:

$$P(\Psi_t|\varphi_{\Phi_t}(\Delta_t^{i(j)})) = S_t^{\Delta^i} = \frac{\rho}{\ell \times (\mu + 1)} \quad , \tag{5.6}$$

where ρ and μ denote the number of matched points between ROI_0^i and $ROI_t^{i(j)}$ and the average of pixel displacement field, respectively. Since the number of extracted keypoints from an image is highly related to its size, the similarity function 5.6 is stabilised with the diagonal length of $ROI_t^{i(j)}$ (ℓ). Figure 5.6 illustrates the matching process of the ith object given its valid appearance ROI_0^i. For each update proposal $\Delta_t^{i(j)}$, the region defined by the projection function φ_{Φ_t} ($ROI_t^{i(j)}$) is resized to be the same size as the input data corresponding to the same object (ROI_0^i). In the example of Figure 5.6, the keypoints extracted from ROI_0^i and $ROI_t^{i(j)}$ are marked as (∘) and (+), respectively. Thus the best match is related to the highest number of matched points and the smallest average of pixel displacements. The observation of Δ^i is highly influenced by its appearance on the image plane, where many criteria can control the similarity computation.

The movement of an object Δ_t^i over time frequently causes a perturbation in its appearance. Moreover, light illumination is also an important factor in the change of Δ_t^i's appearance from its first appearance in the scene. According to the significant change of its appearance on the image plane over time, the valid appearance ROI_0^i corresponding to the

$$ROI_0^i \qquad ROI_t^{i(best)} \qquad ROI_t^{i(random)}$$

Figure 5.6: An illustration of matching between ROI_0^i and two update proposals (best proposal $ROI_t^{i(best)}$ and random proposal $ROI_t^{i(random)}$) at the current frame t.

i^{th} object is regularly updated in order to adaptively follow its latest appearance. However, this can happen only if its appearances in two consecutive frames are very similar.

Besides, Δ_t^i may leave the scene or be occluded by other objects, and hence low similarity is measured, concluding an object death. To overcome this, the position of Δ^i is conscientiously estimated and its identity is maintained even if it is not visually tracked for a certain period of time. With this, Δ^i can easily be reintegrated into the scene or gradually leave. The observation likelihood is then:

$$
\begin{aligned}
P(\Psi_t|\varphi_{\Phi_t}(\Delta_t^i)) &= \max\left(S_t^{\Delta^i}, \tilde{S}_t^{\Delta^i}\right) \quad, \\
\tilde{S}_t^{\Delta^i} &= S_{t-1}^{\Delta^i} \times (0.9 - u_t^{\Delta^i}) \quad, \\
u_t^{\Delta^i} &= \begin{cases} u_{t-1}^{\Delta^i} + 0.07 & \text{if } P(\Psi_{t-1}|\varphi_{\Phi_{t-1}}(\Delta_{t-1}^i)) > S_t^{\Delta^i} \\ 0 & \text{Otherwise} \end{cases} \quad,
\end{aligned}
\tag{5.7}
$$

where the parameter $u_t^{\Delta^i}$ increments if the observation of the object Δ^i decreases between the two instances $t-1$ and t. $u_t^{\Delta^i}$ is initialised to 0 at the first appearance of Δ^i and once its observation likelihood increases.

Equation 5.7 makes the moderation characterise the observation likelihood. If the object distinctly appears in im_t, the observation likelihood adopts the current object similarity in order to increase the certainty of its localisation. Otherwise, the object is assumed to be leaving the scene. In other words, the position of the object is estimated based on its motion, where the observation likelihood $P(\Psi_t|\varphi_{\Phi_t}(\Delta_t^i))$ is gradually decreasing in order to maintain the fluency of object leaving. This can be measured by comparing the similarity $S_t^{\Delta^i}$ with the previous observation likelihood $P(\Psi_{t-1}|\varphi_{\Phi_{t-1}}(\Delta_{t-1}^i))$. This functionality also helps when the updat hypothesis is not projected onto the image plane (when $S_t^{\Delta^i} \simeq 0$), so that objects are allowed to leave the scene for a certain period. Below, the projection function from the real world onto the image plane and its inverse are given:

5.3.2.1 Proposal Projection

Basically, an object proposal (update or birth) characterises the position of the object in the real world, where φ_{Φ_t} projects the object hypothesis from the camera coordinates (real world) onto the image coordinates (image plane) given its depth, and real size w.r.t camera parameters as shown in Fig 5.7. Given the position of the tth object $\left(\Delta_t^i = [X, Y, Z]^T\right)$ and the camera parameters $\left(\Phi_t = [T, R]^T\right)$ at time t, the projection function is defined as:

$$\varphi_{\Phi_t}(M; T_t, R_t) = \begin{bmatrix} x \\ y \end{bmatrix} = \begin{bmatrix} \frac{f(X - Z\tan(\alpha))}{X\tan(\alpha) + Z} \\ \frac{f(Y - Z\tan(\beta))}{Y\tan(\beta) + Z} \end{bmatrix} \quad , \tag{5.8}$$

where $M(X, Y, Z) \in \Delta^i$ is any point in the 3D space, while α and β denote the yaw and pitch angles of the camera, respectively.

In the first frame or when a new object is detected, the bounding boxes are projected into the real world given their coordinates on the image plane and using the inverse projection function. Since all objects are assumed to be located on the ground and their real sizes (height and width) are available (Section 5.2), the perpendicular distance between the optical centre and the top of the object (Y) is used to compute the inverse projection function as follows:

$$\varphi_{\Phi_t}^{-1}(\{x, y\}; T_t, R_t) = \begin{bmatrix} X \\ Y \\ Z \end{bmatrix} = \begin{bmatrix} \frac{Z(f\tan(\alpha) + y)}{f - y\tan(\alpha)} \\ Y \\ \frac{Y(f - x\tan(\beta))}{f\tan(\beta) + x} \end{bmatrix} \quad , \tag{5.9}$$

where x is the top of the bounding box that defines the object and y is the horizontal centre of the bounding box. First, Z is computed in function of Y, and then X in terms of Z.

5.4 Motion Model

Since both the objects and the camera are assumed to move smoothly in the space, it is easier for the system to generate reliable proposals. Specifically, The smoothness between configurations $\Theta_{0:t}$ through time is controlled by the second term of Equation 5.1, which is defined by the product of camera motion and objects' motions as follows:

$$P(\Theta_t | \Theta_{t-1}) = P(\Phi_t | \Phi_{t-1}) P(\Delta_t | \Delta_{t-1}) \quad . \tag{5.10}$$

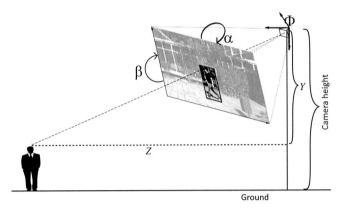

Figure 5.7: An illustration of projection from image coordinate into camera coordinate and vice versa w.r.t camera parameters Φ.

5.4.1 Camera Motion

In normal scenarios, the camera is set up in such a manner to acquire a coherent and understandable scene, by moving as smoothly as possible. However, the environment map, its characteristics and also other moving objects yield irregular changes in its translation and rotation. Unlike [CPS13] which assumes a constant velocity of the camera in the whole video, a smooth change is assumed in its velocity over time [BSG17b].

As mentioned in Section 5.3.1, the estimated translation ($\hat{T}_t$) is deviated from the actual one T_t ($T_t = \hat{T}_t \times s_t$) by a scale factor s_t. Literally, the camera motion controls the scale factor based on the displacement of the camera on the axis with the highest movement. Given the last position of the camera T_{t-1} and its velocity $\dot{T}_t$ (the difference between the two last camera positions), $P(\Phi_t|\Phi_{t-1})$ is modelled by a normal distribution, whose mean is the scale factor s_t, and can be written as follows:

$$P(\Phi_t|\Phi_{t-1}) = \mathcal{N}\left(\frac{T_{t-1}(e) + \dot{T}_t(e)}{\max\left(\hat{T}_t\right)}, 1 \right) \quad , \dot{T}_t = T_{t-1} - T_{t-2} \quad , \tag{5.11}$$

where e denotes the axis taking the maximum movement (i.e. $\max(\hat{T}_t)$).

5.4.2 Object Motion

Objects are assumed to move smoothly and systematically in the space. However, their movements rely on several criteria, such as their dynamic ability (e.g., velocity) and their physical nature (e.g., two objects cannot occupy the same space at the same time). Furthermore, objects have a mutual influence to maintain a safe distance from each other while moving. Arguably, each object determines an area of influence, in which it can allow or exclude other objects [BSG17a]. The intensity and the breadth of the influence are related to the nature of the object and its velocity, where faster objects have the largest front areas of influence. The object motion then becomes:

$$P(\Delta_t|\Delta_{t-1}) = P_{Independent}(\Delta_t|\Delta_{t-1})\, P_{Interation}(\Delta_t|\Delta_{t-1}) \quad . \tag{5.12}$$

In the above equation, $P_{Interation}$ controls the interaction between objects, while $P_{Independent}$ controls their independent movements. Each model is presented as follows:

5.4.2.1 Independent motion

By assuming that objects move smoothly with rational changes, the independent motion distribution $P_{Independent}(\Delta_t|\Delta_{t-1})$ is modelled based on the first-order AutoRegressive (AR) process. At $t = 0$, each object Δ^i is assigned with its initial velocity $\left(v_0^{\Delta^i} = [v^x, v^y, v^z]^{\mathsf{T}}\right)$ based on its category (e.g., a car is supposed to be faster than a pedestrian). Subsequently, the velocity is updated as $v_t^{\Delta^i} = v_{t-1}^{\Delta^i} - v_{t-2}^{\Delta^i}$. On this basis, the independent motion of the Δ_t^i's 3D position at time t is modelled by the following normal distribution having the peak at $\Delta_{t-1}^i + v_t^{\Delta^i}$:

$$P_{Independent}(\Delta_t^i|\Delta_{t-1}^i) = \mathcal{N}\left(\Delta_{t-1}^i + v_t^{\Delta^i}, 1\right) \quad . \tag{5.13}$$

5.4.2.2 Interaction motion

In practice, several criteria can affect the interactions between two objects. However, the nature of the objects themselves is the most significant one. For example, people can move in groups contrary to vehicles, though, they both move on specific paths. Moreover, the interaction of individuals usually develops over time, where for example, two pedestrians can move together for a certain period of time then get separated. In addition, the velocity is an important factor, which influences other objects, where fast ones expel the others in front.

For two objects Δ_t^{i1} and Δ_t^{i2} at time t, two modes of interaction motions called *Repulsion* and *Group* are modelled using MRF. Since a pair of objects is not assumed to remain the same interaction characteristic all the time, a hidden variable σ is employed in order to switch between the two modes. For this, a potential switch of the interaction exists at each time t by computing the probability of both repulsion and group (Equation 5.16 and Equation 5.17) based on the interaction model (Equation 5.15) previously approved. The interaction motion can be represented as follows:

$$P_{Interaction}(\Delta_t | \Delta_{t-1}) = \prod_{t1 < t2} \omega(\Delta_t^{t1}, \Delta_t^{t2}; \sigma_t^{\Delta^{t1}, \Delta^{t2}}) \quad , \tag{5.14}$$

where $\omega(\Delta_t^{t1}, \Delta_t^{t2}; \sigma_t^{\Delta^{t1}, \Delta^{t2}})$ is a probability mode of Δ_t^{t1} and Δ_t^{t2} based on the binary variable $\sigma_t^{\Delta^{t1}, \Delta^{t2}}$ (repulsion = "1" or group = "2"). Here, $\sigma_t^{\Delta^{t1}, \Delta^{t2}}$ is determined as the mode that is more probable for time t having the highest weight among both modes:

$$\sigma_t^{\Delta^{t1}, \Delta^{t2}} = \text{argmax}(r_t^{\Delta^{t1}, \Delta^{t2}} \omega(\Delta^{t1}, \Delta^{t2}; 1), \quad g_t^{\Delta^{t1}, \Delta^{t2}} \omega(\Delta^{t1}, \Delta^{t2}; 2)) \quad ,$$

$$\text{where}: \quad \begin{bmatrix} r_t^{\Delta^{t1}, \Delta^{t2}} \\ g_t^{\Delta^{t1}, \Delta^{t2}} \end{bmatrix} = \begin{cases} [0.8, 0.2]^\top & \text{if } \sigma_{t-1}^{\Delta^{t1}, \Delta^{t2}} = 1 \\ [0.2, 0.8]^\top & \text{Otherwise} \end{cases} . \tag{5.15}$$

In order to avoid arbitrary changes, the factors r and g in the above equation maintain the smoothness of the mode toggle over time. In addition, they raise the certainty of the selected mode. *Repulsion* and *group* modes can be computed as follows:

Repulsion mode: This mode pushes apart two objects that are not assumed to form a group, by controlling the spacing between them in the 3D space. Considering $d_t^{\Delta^{t1}, \Delta^{t2}}$ to be the distance between Δ^{t1} and Δ^{t2} in the real world at time t. The repulsion is computed as follows:

$$\omega(\Delta_t^{t1}, \Delta_t^{t2}; 1) = 0.6 \times e^{\frac{-1}{d_t^{\Delta^{t1}, \Delta^{t2}}}} + 0.2 \times (\delta(\Delta_t^{t1}, \Delta_t^{t2}) + \delta(\Delta_t^{t2}, \Delta_t^{t1})) \quad ,$$

$$\delta(\Delta_t^{t1}, \Delta_t^{t2}) = \exp\left(-\log_{10}\left(v_t^{\Delta^{t1}} + 1\right) / \sin\left(\max\left(90, \tau_t^{\Delta^{t1}, \Delta^{t2}}\right)\right)\right) \quad , \tag{5.16}$$

where $\tau_t^{\Delta^{t1}, \Delta^{t2}}$ denotes the angle between the vectors $\overrightarrow{\Delta_t^{t1} \Delta_{t-1}^{t1}}$ and $\overrightarrow{\Delta_t^{t1} \Delta_t^{t2}}$ as illustrated in Figure 5.8. According to Equation5.16, the repulsion between two objects is high when the distance between them is large and their velocities are low as can be seen in Figure 5.9. Additionally, the repulsion is influenced by the acuteness of the angle τ in order to expels object in the front.

Group mode: This mode controls the rapprochement of objects which are supposed to move together. In the group mode, objects keep moving with similar velocities and

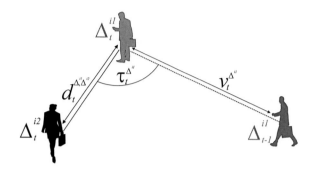

Figure 5.8: An illustration of the repulsion mode in the interaction model.

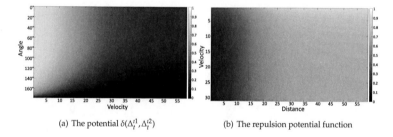

(a) The potential $\delta(\Delta_t^{i1}, \Delta_t^{i2})$

(b) The repulsion potential function

Figure 5.9: **Left:** The potential $\delta(\Delta_t^{i1}, \Delta_t^{i2})$, generated in function of $v_t^{\Delta^{i1}}$ and $\tau_t^{\Delta^{i1}, \Delta^{i2}}$. **Right:** The potential function for the repulsion interaction that is generated in function of the distance between objects and their velocity. The potentials are generated in this example by assuming that both objects have the same variable velocity and both angles are 30°

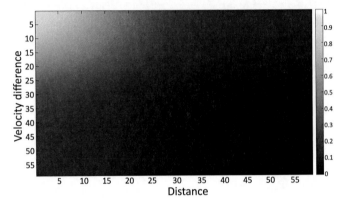

Figure 5.10: The potential function for group interaction, generated in function of the distance between objects and the velocity difference.

close distance. Assuming that the distance controls the direction of both objects, the group probability is:

$$\omega(\Delta_t^{i1}, \Delta_t^{i2}; 2) = \frac{e^{-\log_{10}\left(|v_t^{\Delta^{i1}} - v_t^{\Delta^{i2}}| + 1\right)}}{\sqrt{d_t^{\Delta^{i1}, \Delta^{i2}}}} \quad . \tag{5.17}$$

Equation 5.17 means that a group has an inverse relationship with separation distance and velocity difference. This means that a low velocity difference and small separation distance result in a high group potential and vice-versa as shown in Figure 5.10.

5.5   Sampling

In order to approximate the best configuration, N proposals are generated and validated. Given the configuration Θ_{t-1} that consists of existing objects at $t-1$, the sampling process starts with a random configuration $\Theta_t^{j=0}$. Afterwards, it iteratively jumps to a new one Θ_t^{j+1} until $j = N$, where the validation criterion accepts the jump if the generated configuration is better than its former. Precisely, this process randomly selects a jump model among a pre-defined set of reversible models each of which is reversible to each other or to itself, where only one can be applied for each sampling step. This reversibility means that every model must have a corresponding reverse one, e.g., *Birth* and *Death* counteract each other. The purpose is to deny a proposal after a certain interval so that the jump chain approaches the best configuration and generate balanced proposals [KBD05]. Moreover, the jump model permits to select one of the objects to be considered arbitrarily. The aim of the sampling process is to effectively cover the probability distribution of Θ_t, whose dimensionality is high and variable, where a jump model may either extend Θ_t's dimension (Object Birth), decrease it (Object Death) or keep the same dimensionality (Object Update). Following the Metropolis-Hastings algorithm [Has70], the acceptance ratio of the jump from Θ_t^j to Θ_t^{j+1} is computed as follows:

$$A = \frac{P(\Psi_t|\Theta_t^{j+1})}{P(\Psi_t|\Theta_t^j)} \frac{P(\Theta_t^{j+1}|\Psi_{0,..,t-1})}{P(\Theta_t^j|\Psi_{0,..,t-1})} \frac{Q(\Theta_t^j;\Theta_t^{j+1})}{Q(\Theta_t^{j+1};\Theta_t^j)} \quad , \tag{5.18}$$

where A is the product of three terms: 1) The ratio between observation models, 2) The ratio between posteriori probabilities, 3) The ratio between proposal distributions. A proposal Θ_t^{j+1} is accepted only if $A \geq 1$, otherwise it is rejected and is substituted with Θ_t^j ($\Theta_t^{j+1} = \Theta_t^j$). Each jump model is described by denoting the last hypothesis at $t-1$ and the jth hypothesis at t by Θ_{t-1} and Θ_t^j, respectively.

5.5.1 Object Birth

The birth model adds a new object that did not exist neither in Δ_{t-1} nor in $\Delta_t^{\mathfrak{E}}$ to the set of object Δ_t^{j+1}. First, an object category is randomly proposed. Afterwards, a 3D position and a size are assigned based on the distribution of objects in the space. In this respect, it is important to ensure that the projection onto the image plane falls completely within the image boundary. The corresponding bounding box is evaluated using the object detector [Fel+10], which provides a binary output $V(\Delta^{new})$ denoting the value of the detection confidence $[0,1]$ (0: not detected, 1: certainly detected). However, the projection of the proposed bounding box might be bigger than the detected one or does not completely cover the object. Consequently, the detected bounding box goes through the same phases as the first frame, where the proposed position and size are neglected. For k existing objects from the previous frame to the current sample, the proposal distribution then becomes:

$$Q_B(\Delta_t^{j+1};\Delta_t^j) = \begin{cases} e^{\log_{10}\left(\bar{d}(\Delta^{new},\Delta)-\check{S}(\Delta^{new},\Delta)\right)}, & \text{if} \quad V(\Delta^{new}) = 1 \\ 0 & \text{Otherwise} \end{cases} \quad ,$$

$$\text{where}: \begin{array}{l} \bar{d}(\Delta^{new},\Delta) = \min_{i=1}^k \left(d(\Delta^{new},\Delta^i)\right) \quad , \\ \check{S}(\Delta^{new},\Delta) = \max_{i=1}^k \left(S(\Delta^{new},\Delta^i)\right) \quad . \end{array} \tag{5.19}$$

In Equation 5.19, $\bar{d}$ denotes the distance between the newly added object Δ^{new} and its closest one among Δ_t. Here, it is assumed that new objects are potentially distant from others, although they may form a group with some of them. In addition, $\check{S}$ is computed based on Equation 5.6 and denotes the maximum similarity between the projection of Δ^{new} and the projection of each object in Δ_t. This ensures that the newly proposed object does not overtake the state of an existing object. In order to generate a reasonable number of birth models, only one object is allowed to enter the scene at each time t. After the first generation, the birth model is applied only if the chain moves back to the previous hypothesis (Object Death).

5.5.2   Object Death

As the reversible jump for the birth proposal, the death proposal is applied to an object that belongs to Δ_t^j but not to Δ_{t-1}. The distribution of death proposal is expressed by the maximum similarity between the projection of the newly added object $\Delta_t^{new(j+1)}$ and the last valid appearances of the remaining objects in Δ_t^j:

$$Q_D(\Delta_t^{j+1}; \Delta_t^j) = \begin{cases} e^{\frac{-1}{d(\Delta^{new},\Delta_t)} \times (1-\check{S}(\Delta_t^{new},\Delta_t))^2} & if\, v(\Delta_t^{new}) = 1 \\ 0 & Otherwise \end{cases} \qquad (5.20)$$

5.5.3   Object Stay

This model reinserts a randomly selected object Δ^i from the set $\epsilon_t^{S(j)}$ that contains objects, which are no longer in Δ_t^j but existed in Δ_{t-1}. For a more robust reinsertion, a new position of Δ^i is proposed based on its previous position at $t-1$, ensuring that it is different from that in its last existence at t. Stay proposal distribution is written as follows:

$$Q_S(\Delta_t^{j+1}; \Delta_t^j) = \begin{cases} \frac{1}{|\epsilon_t^{S(j)}|} P(\Psi_t|\varphi_{\Phi_t}(\Delta_t^{i(j+1)})) & if\, \iota \in \epsilon_t^{S(j)} \\ 0 & Otherwise \end{cases} \qquad (5.21)$$

where $P(\Psi_t|\varphi_{\Phi_t}(\Delta_t^{i(j+1)}))$ is the observation likelihood of Δ^i in the newly sampled Δ_t^{j+1}.

5.5.4   Object Exit

The reversible jump of stay proposes to remove a randomly selected object from $\epsilon_t^{L(j)}$, which is the set of objects that belongs to Δ_t^j but not to Δ_{t-1}. The proposal is then:

$$Q_L(\Delta_t^{j+1}; \Delta_t^j) = \begin{cases} \frac{1}{|\epsilon_t^{L(j)}|} & if\, \iota \in \epsilon_t^{L(j)} \\ 0 & Otherwise \end{cases} \qquad (5.22)$$

5.5.5 Object Update

The update jump proposes a new position of an object $\Delta_t^{i,j+1}$, which is randomly selected from the set of objects in Δ_t^j. It has to be noted that a newly added object at t is excluded from this set. The update model is auto-reversible (reversed by another update jump), and searches for a better position of a given object. Thus, the Metropolis Hastings becomes a random walk algorithm by considering a symmetric distribution for the update proposal. In this context, the update mode is controlled only with the motion model and the observation likelihood. The proposal distribution is then modelled by a simple normal distribution, where the mean is the current position $\Delta_t^{i,j}$ of the ith object and the variance is one: $Q_U(\Delta_t^{i,j+1}; \Delta_t^{i,j}) = \mathcal{N}(\Delta_t^{i,j+1}, 1)$.

5.5.6 Camera Update

Similarly to object update, camera update is modelled by a normal distribution, where it is reversed to another camera update. The proposal can be written using the current camera position Φ_t^j as the mean of a normal distribution: $Q_U(\Phi_t^{j+1}; \Phi_t^j) = \mathcal{N}(\Phi_t^{j+1}, 1)$.

5.6 Summary

In this chapter, a sub-framework for 3D trajectory extraction is introduced [BSG17a]. Here, the purpose is to analyse uncalibrated monocular moving videos to simultaneously localise both the camera and the objects in the real world. This is handled by adopting an example-based approach to compensate the lack of information. Specifically, the intrinsic parameters of the camera (i.e., focal length) and the depths of the objects are estimated in order to initialise the system in the first frame. Subsequently, with the help of RJ-MCMC particle filtering, the 3D trajectories of the camera and the objects are estimated. In this regard, it is assumed that the previous positions of a given object and the evolution of motion (sequence of positional changes over time [KSS07]) indicate the current and following positions of the object. For an accurate localisation of objects, their interaction is studied to maintain their identities as long as they are tracked. For camera odometry, the example-based approach is extended to estimate the depths of segments that are on planar surfaces. The aim of this estimation is to use the obtained depths as a cue implying the movements of the camera [BSG17b]. Overall, this chapter contributes to compensate the lack of information in uncalibrated monocular moving videos. In addition to localising the camera and the objects in the real world. The sub-framework presented in this chapter is qualitatively and quantitatively evaluated in Section 7.2.2 and Section 7.3.

Chapter 6

Application: Trajectory Analysis

Analysing human activities in crowded scenes is a challenging task due to several factors. Notably, the vast diversity of possible activities makes their recognition very complex due to the high inter-class similarity and in some cases a low intra-class similarity. Moreover, the main difficulty in crowd scenarios is the tangled trajectories, with which activities are hard to be characterised. Specifically, not only the activity of an individual, which defines its path but also other moving objects, stationary objects and rigid obstacles. This means that even with the assumption that trajectories have a high discriminative power to recognise different activities, there exist other external factors that have a strong influence in the determination of trajectories. Considering those factors, this chapter addresses two important applications of analysing the activities of pedestrians based on their trajectories in crowded environments.

6.1   Convoy Detection

The idea of this section is similar to the extant studies [JSZ08; Jeu+08]. However, contrary to most of the methods, which analyse the activities of people's group by considering multi-patterns (e.g., uniform, stable, conflict, etc.) [SLW14], this work focuses only on detecting convoys, with a new proposed pattern called *non-continuous convoy* [Bou+16a]. This limitation is due to the confusing output of the multitude of patterns since the difference between their properties is intangible and difficult to be defined. In addition, the diversity of patterns is not assumed to have a high contribution to understanding people group activities.

The difficulty of detecting convoys increases as the density of people is high, where patterns change their intra-properties (e.g., relative positions of pedestrians in one group) and inter-properties (e.g., crossing groups) over time. Therefore, a two-phase algorithm is proposed to detect groups of pedestrians "*Convoy*" [Bou+16a], where the first phase named "*density clustering*" is robust to the development of the intra-properties of pedestrians. Notably, if the relative positions of pedestrians in a group changed, this functionality allows them to stay in the same group as long as they are densely connected. The second phase (*intersection phase*) addresses the inter-properties by iteratively intersecting groups of pedestrians. Here, a set of pedestrians is regarded as a convoy, provided that its elements continuously compose a group over a sequence. In the following, *convoy* is defined and the the clustering/intersection method for convoy detection is explained:

6.1.1 Noncontinuous Convoy:

A convoy can be defined as a group of objects which are *density-connected* with each other during a certain period of time [JSZ08]. In this context, "*density-connected*" determines whether the members (object) of a cluster are spatially together, by continuously measuring their intra-properties. However, in real scenarios, convoys do not consistently enjoy this property due to the high constraint of consecutiveness. For example, an obstacle is an important factor that separates two moving pedestrians for a certain time. Furthermore, one or more pedestrian(s) in one convoy may be imprecisely tracked. Hence, it is not density-connected with others in the same convoy, and obviously, it is assumed to be out the convoy.

For this issue, a pattern called "non-continuous convoy" is defined, which is characterised by the relaxation of consecutiveness. In other words, a convoy exists and gather its members as long as they are not separated for a long period. Arguably, the method is reasonable tolerant for short separations, where a convoy rationally persists until its members get back together. In order to determine the tolerable distance of separation, A parameter called *Elasticity* (ξ) is adopted, and computed as follows:

$$\xi = \min_{i=1}^{C}\left(\frac{l_i'}{l_i}\right) \quad , \tag{6.1}$$

where l' and l denote the sum of lengths of density-connected frames and the total duration of the convoy (non-continuous), respectively. C represents the number of training convoys. Equation 6.1 means that a convoy is entirely continuous only if $\xi = 1$. Meanwhile, $\xi = 0.5$ means that the members of a convoy are density-connected in more than half of the convoy's duration.

6.1.2 Clustering and Intersection:

To employ trajectories in the detection of convoys, a two-phases algorithm is implemented, which consists of a clustering phase and an intersection phase. Figure 6.1 shows an example

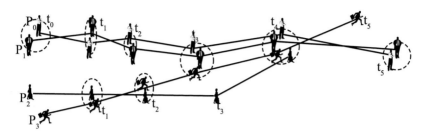

	t_0	t_1	t_2	t_3	t_4	t_5
Clusters	(p_0, p_1)	(p_0, p_1) (p_2, p_3)	(p_0, p_1) (p_2, p_3)	(p_0, p_1, p_3)	(p_0, p_1, p_2, p_3)	(p_0, p_1)
Candidates	(p_0, p_1), 1	(p_0, p_1), 2 (p_2, p_3), 1	*(p_0, p_1), 3* (p_2, p_3), 2	*(p_0, p_1), 4* (p_0, p_1, p_3), 1	*(p_0, p_1), 5* (p_0, p_1, p_3), 2 (p_0, p_1, p_2, p_3), 1	*(p_0, p_1), 6*
Convoy			(p_0, p_1), 3	(p_0, p_1), 4	(p_0, p_1), 5	(p_0, p_1), 6

Figure 6.1: An illustration of convoy detection.

case of 4 pedestrians. Initially, convoy candidates are formed based on the spatial distance between their members at time t_0 [Est+96]. Once the duration of gathering members is long enough (reaches or exceeds the predefined threshold), a convoy is validated. However, the members of a convoy may partly get separated over time due to the intersection with other objects as shown in Figure 6.1. In this example, a convoy candidate denoted as '$(\Delta^{i1}, p^{i2})_{L'}$' means that Δ^{i1} and Δ^{i2} are density-connected for L' frames. At each time $t > 0$, a convoy candidate that is formed at $t-1$ becomes the intersection result of its members at time $t-1$ and clusters at time t. Finally, a convoy candidate exceeding the duration threshold (in italic font) is validated as a convoy, where in this example, the minimum length of a convoy is set up to two frames, and the minimum number of members is two.

6.1.3 Candidate Expiring Mechanism:

In order to detect non-continuous convoys, an expiring mechanism is used, whose goal is to avoid unlikely inflation/deflation of a candidate's set. In simpler words, a candidate with a density-connected length smaller than the threshold is not removed immediately. Rather, the length of its apparent existence and that of its possible disappearance are compared to the formerly computed ξ. For this, the disappearance rate a_i for each ith candidate is compared with ξ, where the candidate is removed only if $a_i \leq \xi$. The disappearance rate a_i^{th} for the th candidate is computed as follows:

$$a_i = \frac{l'_i}{t_{current}^i - t_{birth}^i} \quad , \tag{6.2}$$

where l' denotes the sum of lengths of density-connected frames. $t_{current}$ and t_{birth} are the current frame and the first existing frame of the corresponding candidate, respectively.

Algorithm 3 presents a detailed explanation of both the clustering and intersection phases, including the candidate expiring mechanism. First, a density-based clustering algorithm (DBSCAN) [Est+96] is performed for all objects in each frame (line 1-3), where the output consists of clusters of density-connected members. Next, candidates are initialised, where all clusters are added to the set of candidates R (line 4-7), if no candidate is assumed to exist. Subsequently, the algorithm refines the candidates by intersecting them with the new clusters (line 8-11). An intersection result that contains in addition to a previous convoy candidate, new members, is considered as a new candidate born currently (different from the previous one) (line 12-14). Here, the new clusters are added to R (line 15), which is regularly updated (line 16). In each iteration, the algorithm evaluates the elasticity of the existing candidates. If a candidate exceeds the duration threshold, it is output as a convoy (line 17-19). Meanwhile, a candidate is discarded if it does not satisfy the elasticity criteria (line 20-21).

6.2   Suspicious Activity Detection

Basically, normal and abnormal activities cannot be characterised, where the abnormality is defined as "atypical behaviour patterns that are not represented by sufficient samples in a training dataset but critically they satisfy the specificity constraint to abnormal patterns." [XG05]. This means that abnormal activities are assumed to occur rarely compared to normal ones, which form the range of activities being performed by most people. However, the normality/abnormality concept changes depending on several criteria, where Xiang and Gong [XG08] assume that this concept is "highly dependent on the visual context and can change over time". They add: "a behaviour can be considered as either being normal or abnormal depending on when and where it takes place" [XG08]. Hence, it is futile to train a classifier using labelled normal and abnormal activities, since the characteristics of both may change. In addition, detecting such activities of people require a high-level information that describes the local movements of pedestrians. However, these kinds of information are not

---

Algorithm 3: Clustering and Intersection

Data: cluster size threshold m, duration threshold k, DBSCAN distance threshold e,
DBSCAN density threshold u and sequenced trajectory data frame$S$

Result: convoys that reached the thresholds

1 **for** *frame s in S* **do**

2   initialize empty set R';

3   cluster the objects in s with respect to e and u;

4   **if** $R = \emptyset$ **then**

5   **for** *cluster c in s* **do**

6   add c to R;

7   continue;

8   **for** *cluster r in R* **do**

9   **for** *cluster c in s* **do**

10   new candidate $r' = r \cap c$;

11            $duration(r') = duration(r) + duration(s)$;

12   **if** $size(r') \geq m$ **then**

13                $createdTime(r') = currentTime$;

14   add r' to R';

15   add c to R';

16   add R' to R;

17   **for** *cluster r in R* **do**

18   **if** $duration(r) \geq k$ **then**

19   output r as a qualified convoy;

20   **if** $duration(r)/(currentTime - cureatedTime(r)) \leq l$ **then**

21   remove r from R;

---

available in surveillance videos due to the crowd density and the low resolution. Moreover, even if they are available, their automatic extraction is extremely hard and time consuming. In this work, only trajectories are assumed to be accessible, which can highly characterise normal activities, but not abnormal ones. For better perception, considering a fictional trajectory extracted in the train station, where its executor is running in all directions, trying to not miss his/her train by finding the appropriate gate. Here, the activity is obviously normal. However, for the same trajectory taken in the same location and under the same conditions (e.g., time, crowd density, etc.), but its executor is a thief, who is running to avoid being arrested. This activity is abnormal, although, its trajectory is completely similar to that of a normal activity. For this reason, "abnormal" is replaced with "suspicious" in this work in order to avoid any ambiguity.

For the issue mentioned above, a modified Positive Unlabelled (PU) learning approach is proposed to prepare the training data that consists of reliable normal (defined as "positive") and suspicious (defined as "negative") activity examples. Both parts are extracted from an unlabeled data based on a very limited positive set. The output is used after that to train a Two-Class SVM in order to classify activities that subject to the same specifications of the training data. Accordingly, discriminative characteristics are extracted from all trajectories, where the velocity and the path direction are assumed to express this discrimination. The extracted characteristics are as follows:

Displacement: Generally, people move consistently in the real world, having a clear target and trying to keep a straight path. Therefore, the displacement of an object is computed at each time t'_l of its existing life in the scene. Precisely, the displacement denotes the euclidean distance between the starting point and the point reached at t'_l.

Distance: Despite the assumed straightness of the paths of people, a pedestrian frequently moves longer than its actual displacement due to external and internal factors (e.g., obstacles and physical ability). However, he/she spontaneously tries to keep the distance as shorter as possible. Consequently, its distance is measured at each time t'_l and denotes the travelled distance along the actual path from the starting point until the current point. The difference between *displacement* and *distance* can be seen in Fig 6.2.

Velocity: The time consumed to travel between two points on a straight line (regardless the actual path) is usually in a specific range (e.g., the displacement between two gates in the train station). Therefore, this characteristic is the velocity measurement at each time t, which is the ratio of the displacement until t'_l to the travelling time.

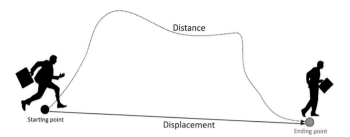

Figure 6.2: The difference between *displacement* and *distance*, where the displacement is the euclidean distance between two points and the distance is the travelled distance along the actual path.

Instantaneous Speed: Although a pedestrian is not assumed to have a constant speed all the time, the change in his/her velocity should be relatively stable. In this sense, this characteristic measures the speed between each consecutive frames, which is simply the euclidean distance between the position at time t'_i and that at $t'_i - 1$.

Speed: Similarly to the velocity, the consumed time to travel between two points on the actual path is assumed to be in a specific range. Precisely, even if the pedestrian increases or decreases his/her instantaneous speed for a while, the overall speed should not remarkably deviate from the normal cases. The speed characteristic of a pedestrian is then the ratio of his/her distance until the current frame t'_i to the travelling time.

Path Direction: In well-known areas, possible paths, on which people may move, are relatively analogous (e.g., from the counter to the gate in the train station). For this, the positions of a pedestrian on both axes (X and Z) are considered separated characteristics by initialising the starting point (X and Z) to 0 so that the paths are homogeneous.

At each time t in the video sequence, the above characteristics are computed for all existing objects based on their trajectories. Given a trajectory $\Delta_{0:t'_i}^t$ that exists for $t'_i \leq t$ frames, the corresponding initial descriptor $F_{t'_i}^t$ is then the concatenation of all characteristics, which are sequentially computed from the first frame of the appearance to the current one. Since the lengths of trajectories are not equal, the extracted features are interpolated to have a specific length. Here, the dimension of each characteristic vector becomes 10 and thus the dimension of the whole feature vector is 70. In addition, the trajectory is considered only after 10 frames of its existence.

Besides, higher-level descriptors can also be extracted from the initial ones using code-

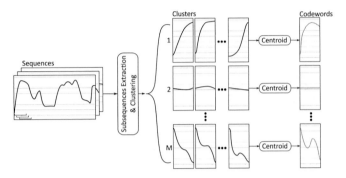

Figure 6.3: An overview of codebook construction.

book approach, which represents the sequence as a distribution of characteristic subsequences [SKG16]. Since each characteristic in the initial descriptor denotes a measurement sequence, a high-level feature descriptor $(F'^{l}_{l'_i})$ can be extracted from $F^{l}_{l'_i}$ representing histograms of formerly collected words. This approach consists of two phases, where the first one that is illustrated in Figure 6.3 is to construct the codebook. Considering one characteristic among the presented above, all possible subsequences are collected from each sequence with a similar length v. Then, *k-means* [Llo06] is performed in order to obtain M clusters, whose centroids are the codewords.

The second phase is illustrated in Figure 6.4 and is dedicated to obtain $F'^{l}_{l'_i}$. For each characteristic sequence in $F^{l}_{l'_i}$, all possible windows are extracted with the length v. Afterwards, the occurrence frequency of each codeword in the initial sequence is computed, where the extracted window adopts the closest codeword based on the euclidean distance. Consequently, the dimension of the whole feature vector $(F'^{l}_{l'_i})$ is $M \times v$. Additionally, in order to have a homogeneous data, the windows extracted from *Displacement*, *Distance* and *Path Direction* in both phases are initialised to 0. For simplicity, F'_β is used in the remaining of this section to indicate the extracted histogram of the βth trajectory, which is characterised by its executor, its starting time and ending time.

To detect suspicious activities, a semi-supervised approach is proposed to prepare the training data, which is used afterwards to train a Two-Class SVM classifier. The preparation of the training data follows the method proposed by Nguyen *et al.* [NLN11], which identifies the positive and negative boundaries for the ground truth given one positive seed. Figure 6.5 illustrates the process of obtaining normal and suspicious examples considering a set of unlabelled training trajectories ($\mathcal{U}$). First, few trajectories that represent *pure* normal activity are assigned to the positive set $\mathcal{P}$. Next, the euclidean distances between the centroid of

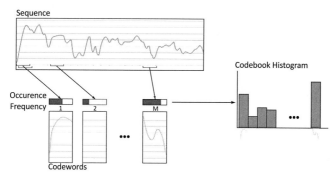

Figure 6.4: An overview of codebook representation.

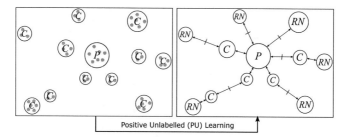

Figure 6.5: An illustration of boundary decision following the steps: (1) Select few positive examples ($\mathcal{P}$) from the unlabelled trajectories (Red dots), (2) Divide the remaining data into (Cs) clusters and (3) Obtain positive and negative examples.

$\mathcal{P}$ and the remaining trajectories of $\mathcal{U}$ are computed. All trajectories that have a smaller distance to the centroid than $\mathcal{P}$'s elements are automatically assigned to $\mathcal{P}$. The set of the remaining trajectories ($\mathcal{U} = \mathcal{U} - \mathcal{P}$) is then divided into small clusters ($C_{1...\mathcal{L}-1}$) using $k\text{-means}$, where the trajectories in each cluster share the same characteristics and are assumed to have a similar class label (Positive "Normal" or Negative "Suspicious"). In this phase, each cluster $\ell = 1 \cdots \mathcal{L}$ (including $\mathcal{P}$) is considered as one entity and is represented by one feature vector which is the centroid of the cluster.

At this point, the data is a set of entities (clusters), among which only one is labelled ($\mathcal{P}$), with the assumption that few entities that denote negative examples exist. Hence, it is necessary to carefully search for negative entities among the $\mathcal{L} - 1$ unlabelled ones, so that the positive examples are not picked. This necessity is justified by the fact that the presence of false negative examples will eventually reduce the performance of the classification. For this purpose, *k-means* clustering is used with $k = 2$ in order to cluster the $\mathcal{L}-1$ entities using their transformed feature vectors $\hat{F}_{1:\mathcal{L}-1}$, where each feature vector F'_ℓ is transformed as follows:

$$\hat{F}_\ell = \left| F'_\ell - F'_{\mathcal{L}} \right| \quad . \tag{6.3}$$

Equation 6.3 transforms all feature vectors based on the distance from $\mathcal{P}$, so that the two output clusters differ in the proximity to $\mathcal{P}$. Here, it is assumed that a cluster with fewer entities is distant from $\mathcal{P}$, and thus its entities are assigned to the reliable negative set $(RN_{1...\mathcal{L}'_1})$.

$\mathcal{P}$ and RN represent the extreme positive and negative examples, and hence they are not sufficient to build a classifier. Therefore, the remaining entities $(C_{1:\mathcal{L}-1-\mathcal{L}'_1} = C_{1:\mathcal{L}-1} - RN_{1:\mathcal{L}'_1})$ are identified to likely positives and likely negatives. Starting from RN, the shortest path to $\mathcal{P}$ passing through $C_{1:\mathcal{L}-1-\mathcal{L}'_1}$ is searched using the euclidean distance. Here, each entity in $C_{1:\mathcal{L}-1-\mathcal{L}'_1}$ is considered in one path only. In order to ensure the involvement of most of the entities without passing directly from RNs to $\mathcal{P}$, the direct distance from RNs to $\mathcal{P}$ is magnified by a parameter $\mu > 1$. For the unlabelled entities that do not belong to any path, they are simply discarded.

Later, each path is broken from the maximal distance between its belonging entities, where those connected to $\mathcal{P}$ are assigned as positives and those connected to RNs are assigned as negatives. Finally, all positive and negative entities are used to build a linear Class SVM classifier. Usually, One-Class classification is adopted to isolate positive examples due to their similarity. However, in this approach, several negative examples are automatically provided. Thus, the usage of both positive and negative examples leads to an accurate separation between the two classes.

6.3 Summary

This chapter presents two example applications of trajectory mining with the objective to recognise convoy and suspicious patterns in crowded scenes. In the first application, the trajectories of pedestrians are analysed in order to extract groups of people called "convoys" [Bou+16a]. The mechanism proposed in this approach ensures the continuity of convoys in the case of irrelevant separation (e.g., caused by obstacles). Moreover, in the second application, the trajectory of an object is encoded in higher-level features, which are afterwards employed to recognise the general behaviour of its performer. For this, a semi-supervised approach (PU learning) is adopted to distinguish abnormal activities from normal ones. The importance of this chapter's contributions lies in the efficient interpretation of pure trajectories into high-level human activities in crowded videos.

Chapter 7

Experiments and Results

In this chapter, the experiments and results of all presented methods in this work are collected for detailed evaluations. For each experiment, the implementation details, used datasets and parameters are introduced at the beginning of the correspondent section. Afterwards, quantitative and qualitative evaluations are presented. Finally, the results are discussed in detail in order to demonstrate the effectiveness and the limitation of the methods.

7.1 Object Detection

For object detection, two experiments are presented corresponding to the methods introduced in Chapter 3. The first evaluation is addressed to validate the detection method in surveillance videos using key-points. The second one validates the method that focuses on detecting objects in still images by selectively searching for reliable candidates.

7.1.1 Object Detection in Surveillance Videos

7.1.1.1 Dataset

Object Detection Dataset (ODD): For the experimental evaluation of key-points-based object detection, the pedestrian walking dataset [YLW15b] is used. The dataset is of about one-hour length containing 12.648 paths of pedestrian, who are walking in different directions. Only 600 frames ($\simeq$ 6 min) are considered in this experiment. In this dataset, each object is annotated with a single point instead of bounding box, due to the small size of pedestrian projections onto the image plane.

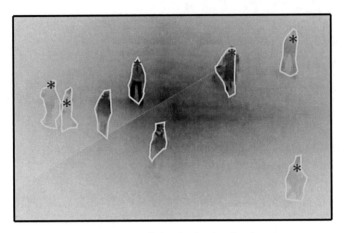

Figure 7.1: An example result of pedestrian detection.

7.1.1.2   Evaluation

For a qualitative assessment, Figure 7.1 illustrates an example result of the pedestrian detection method on *ODD*. The output of the proposed method is represented by boundaries, and the ground truth is represented by (∗)s. In this evaluation, a correct object detection means that the annotated point is surrounded by the output boundary of the method. Otherwise, the detection is considered to be wrong.

Practically, the pedestrian detection method is controlled by several parameters depending on the specifications of the query video. More precisely, the size of a pedestrian bounding box has to be priorly defined. Here, the bounding boxes of all pedestrians in the same video are assumed to relatively have similar sizes. Additionally, the minimum number of feature points is also an important factor that controls the detection sensitivity. For quantitative evaluation, Table 7.1 shows the result of the pedestrian detection using two criteria: the threshold number of key-points and the threshold of pedestrian size. Based on these standards, the precision and the recall are computed for each combination of parameters. Here, *LFT*, *HFT*, *SZT* and *BZT* denote a low threshold of key-point number, a high threshold of key-point number, a small threshold of pedestrian size and a big threshold of pedestrian size, respectively. For example, the corresponding result for *LFT-BZT* is computed with the consideration of a low threshold of key-points and a big threshold of bounding box size. For this combination, among 697 pedestrians existing in the scene, 596 are correctly detected and 164 falsely detected.

The result in the above table shows the effectiveness of the presented detection method

Table 7.1: Pedestrian detection result using 4 different parameter combinations.

	LFT - SZT	HFT - SZT	LFT - BZT	HFT - BZT
Recall	0.97	0.9	0.86	0.79
Precision	0.7	0.74	0.78	0.86

in localising objects in videos of crowded scenarios. Moreover, it demonstrates that a small threshold of bounding box size yields to better result compared to a bigger one. On the other side, the presented result indicates the relative sensitivity of the method to the change of parameters, especially to the threshold size of the pedestrian. This is due to the appearance similarity between pedestrians and other shapes in the scene, where for smaller size other shapes might be considered as pedestrians and thus a low precision. For a bigger size threshold, true positive pedestrians might be miss-detected, in the case where key-points do not cover the whole pedestrian region.

7.1.2 Object Detection in Still Image

7.1.2.1 Dataset

Object Detection Dataset* (ODD*): In order to evaluate the accuracy of the pedestrian detection method, which selectively searches for reliable candidates, ODD* is a part of the pedestrian walking dataset [YLW15b] (described in Section 7.1.1). The first third of this dataset is dedicated to the training part of ODD*. For testing, 100 images are randomly selected from the last two-thirds. For the ground truth of this dataset, pedestrians are labelled only by their position coordinates.

7.1.2.2 Evaluation

The purpose of this evaluation is to validate the capability of the proposed method to detect objects (pedestrians in this work) under strict conditions (low-resolution and crowd). Accordingly, the ground truth of ODD* is processed in a manner that includes the bounding boxes of objects. Precisely, it is assumed that the pedestrians' coordinates denote the *top-centers* of the bounding boxes. Here, the sizes are automatically assigned based on the position on the vertical axis. The reason is that, in the used dataset, the size of a pedestrian's bounding box increases from the top to the bottom of the image. Figure 7.2 displays an example of determining the bounding boxes of the training part, given the position coordinates.

Since the size of a pedestrian bounding box can be estimated, positive (pedestrian) and negative (non-pedestrian) examples are extracted for training, given the predefined

Figure 7.2: An example of bounding boxes determined by position coordinates (red dots).

Table 7.2: Object detection result .

	Precision	Recall
Proposed	**0.795**	**0.648**
Independent	**0.879**	**0.273**

sizes. For testing, the sizes of candidates are determined by the search process. However, to reduce the computational cost, the range of their sizes is priorly defined. Figure 7.3 illustrates two examples of objects detected by the proposed method *"Proposed"* and a state-of-the-art method *"Independent"*[Fel+10]. As clearly demonstrated, *Proposed* can accurately detect objects in crowded scenes compared to *Independent*. In addition, Table 7.2 presents the quantitative results of both methods indicating their precisions and recalls. Specifically, among 2505 pedestrians, *Proposed* precisely detects 1618 with only 425 false alarms. It has to be noted that a correct detection implies that the ground truth and detected bounding boxes overlap for at least 50% of their minimum sizes. Also, in this experiment, only the region which is assumed to contain moving objects is considered.

The presented results demonstrate the capability of the proposed method to detect objects (pedestrians in this experiment) under severe conditions, such as low resolution and crowded environments. Moreover, the comparison analysis indicates, the failure of the classical methods (e.g., [Fel+10]) to detect objects under different settings. On the contrary, *Proposed* is an adjustable method that can easily train a model for new objects.

(a) An example of bounding boxes (associated with their confidance scores) detected by *Proposed*.

(b) An example of bounding boxes detected by *Independent*.

Figure 7.3: Examples of detected bounding boxes.

7.2   3D Trajectory Extraction

This section evaluates and examines the methods and the sub-methods described in both Chapters 4 and 5, which are dedicated to 3D trajectory extraction from surveillance and moving videos, respectively. In the first part, two evaluations are performed showing the result of the extraction method in terms of depth estimation and object detection. In the second part, the main steps of the sub-framework for 3D trajectory extraction from moving videos are evaluated.

7.2.1   3D Trajectory Extraction from Surveillance Videos

7.2.1.1   Dataset

Trajectory Extraction Dataset (TED): This dataset is collected from the *LIRIS* dataset [W*et al.*14], which consists of 180 shots taken by Kinect camera. Explicitly, the dataset is chosen because it allows defining depths of most observed points in the space. Here, the ground truth of objects' depths can be computed by referring to depth maps, which are associated with the RGB images. Each shot in *LIRIS* represents an activity of people, where the camera is placed at different places in a building. In *LIRIS*, several shots do not contain walking pedestrians, and in others, the camera is slightly moving. Therefore, only 80 shots are selected for *TED*, which are down-sampled to 1 fps.

7.2.1.2   Evaluation in terms of Depth Estimation

The goal of this evaluation is to validate the consistency of the extracted 3D trajectories in terms of temporal depths, using the method proposed in Section 4. To this end, the proposed method *"Proposed"* is compared with a state-of-the-art method [KLK16] *"D-Independent"*, which independently estimates the depth map of each frame. In this regard, both methods are performed on *TED*. More precisely, *Proposed* extracts the 3D trajectory of single objects from *TED*, using 700 particles. Afterwards, only the extracted depths are used for the evaluation. This is because the whole trajectory cannot be extracted with *D-Independent*.

The comparison result between *Proposed* and *D-Independent* is presented in Table 7.3, where *d1* denotes the average depth error between the corresponding method and the ground truth. The depth error is computed as the absolute difference between the extracted depth and the ground truth depth. Since the depth deviation in the initial point of a given trajectory affects the entire evaluation of *d1*, *d2* is computed as the average depth error after subtracting the initial depth of the trajectory from *Proposed*, *D-Independent* and the ground truth. Furthermore, $d3$ is computed to evaluate the depth changes that denote the average step deviation. Consequently, depth steps are computed for each two consecutive frames, which means the difference between the depths in these frames. Thus, $d3$ is the average absolute difference between the steps of the corresponding method and those of the ground truth. Table 7.3 demonstrates that *Proposed* significantly outperforms *D-Independent* for all of $d1$, $d2$ and $d3$. Notably, the small depth deviation obtained by *Proposed* ($\approx$ 21 cm) indicates that the estimated step in terms of depth is very similar to the one in the ground truth. This result validates the effectiveness of the proposed method, where 3D trajectories with such properties are practical for video event detection. This is because the interaction of objects is defined as the relation among their relative positions.

	$d1$ (cm)	$d2$ (cm)	$d3$ (cm)
D-Independent	722.709	1052.468	364.175
Proposed	105.862	98.261	21.275

Table 7.3: Performance comparison between *Proposed* and *D-Independent* on *TED* (the unit is millimetre (cm)).

For an intuitive illustration of the achieved result, Figure 7.4 presents three examples of estimated depths obtained by *Proposed*, *D-Independent* and the ground truth. Each graph corresponds to one object in one shot, where the horizontal axis denotes the time stamp, and the vertical one represents the estimated and the ground truth depths. In Figure 7.4, the circles denote the depths estimated by *D-Independent* in the best-selected frame (Section 4.2), from which the object starts to be tracked by the particle filter. As illustrated in Figure 7.4, the estimated depths using *Proposed* are very close to those of the ground truth. On the contrary, the estimated depths using *D-Independent* are unstable. These examples conclude that *Proposed* extracts 3D trajectories with consistent and accurate depths.

Furthermore, two examples of extracted 3D trajectories are shown in Figure 7.5 (a) and (b). The dark trajectory is extracted using *Proposed*, and the bright one is the ground truth trajectory, which is computed in terms of the ground truth depths and manual annotations of object's positions on the image plane. As demonstrated in Figure 7.5, the extracted 3D trajectories are sufficiently similar to those of the ground truth. This result validates the capability of the proposed method in estimating reliable 3D trajectories from 2D videos.

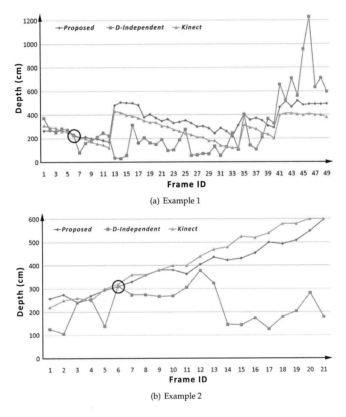

(a) Example 1

(b) Example 2

Figure 7.4: Examples of depths of 3D trajectories obtained by *Proposed*, *D-Independent* and the ground truth (Kinect).

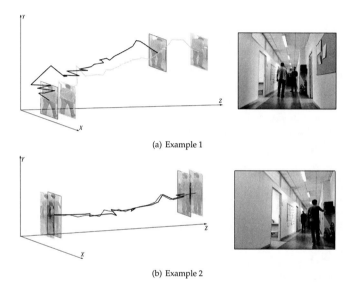

(a) Example 1

(b) Example 2

Figure 7.5: Comparison between 3D trajectories extracted by *Proposed* (dark) and the ground truth (bright).

7.2.1.3   Evaluation in terms of Object Detection

This evaluation focuses on validating the effectiveness of the proposed method in achieving consistent object localisation on the image plane. For this purpose, 30 shots are selected from *TED*, on which the proposed method *"Proposed"* is performed to extract 3D trajectories. Hence, the accuracy of object regions represented by those trajectories is assessed. For a comparison, a state-of-the-art method [Fel+10] is also applied to the same set of shots. The method is called in this section *O-Independent* and is independently applied to each image in a given shot. The results of both methods are presented in Table 7.4. Here, the first row represents the rates of correctly detected regions. The region is correctly detected if it overlaps more than 50% with the provided ground truth, which is manually prepared.

The detected regions which overlap with the ground truth regions for less than 50% are considered incorrectly detected. Hence, the rates of incorrectly detected regions are given in the second row. Literally, the result of this row does not really reflect the accuracy of both methods, where in some cases the regions given by the ground truth are not accurate due to the uncertain appearance of objects' regions, such as the partial occlusion.

Finally, the bottom row indicates the rates of missed regions compared to the ground truth. It is important to remember that *Proposed* tracks the object from the best frame, in which the resolution of the object is usually high enough to detect the object. Afterwards, the high resolution becomes less important since the object region is tracked based on SIFT matching. Besides, the transition distribution at t and the posterior probability at $t-1$ handles the tracking of the object when it is not sufficiently observed. Independently applying *O-Independent* on each frame without considering the existence of the object in the previous frames yields to miss-detect the object under some conditions, such as a low resolution of the object region.

The bottom row indicates the percentage of the ground truth regions that are missed by *Proposed* and *O-Independent*. In tracking applications, there is another important evaluation measure that represents the percentage of 'false positive regions', which do not overlap ground truth ones. However, avoiding false positive regions is not a task of the proposed trajectory extraction method. Rather, it is a task of an object detection method. Therefore, this work does not consider false positive regions.

Although the smallness of the dataset used in this experiment, Table 7.4 demonstrates that *Proposed* accurately tracks objects in the image plane compared to *O-Independent*. Also, no object regions are missed by *Proposed*, which is mainly because the best frame selection step selects frames with clear edges.

	Proposed	O-Independent
Correct regions	85.61 %	69.17 %
Incorrect regions	14.38 %	19.17 %
Missed regions	0 %	11.64 %

Table 7.4: Comparison between *Proposed* and *O-Independent* on 30 videos in *LIRIS* in terms of object detection.

7.2.2   3D Trajectory Extraction from Moving Cameras

In the following experiments, each step in the pipeline of the 3D trajectory extraction method presented in Section 5 is quantitatively evaluated. However, the experiments related to the focal length estimation and camera odometry are not presented in this section, but in the subsequent one. For qualitative evaluation, Figure 7.6 illustrates the overall output of the sub-framework. In this figure, four example of extracted trajectories from Kitti sequences [GLU12] are presented. The bottom images denote the first frames of the sequences, where the last frames are represented by the top images. In the middle, the extracted trajectories of the detected objects and the camera are displayed. In the first example (left), the red car shown in the first frame is tracked for the whole shot (as can be seen as a red circle on the right of the corresponding camera trajectory), although it does not appear in the last frames. Here, the car turned right contrary to the camera. However, the extraction method can deal with unobservable objects for a certain period. Moreover, the ability of the proposed method to track objects in dense regions is demonstrated in the last example of the figure. Below, the datasets used to evaluate the different steps of the proposed method are described. Subsequently, the quantitative results of each of focal length estimation, depth estimation and 3D trajectory extraction are discussed.

7.2.2.1   Datasets

Depth Estimation Dataset (DED): This dataset is dedicated to evaluating the method that estimates the depths of objects. The dataset consists of object images, each of which is annotated with an object category (e.g., Person, Car). Moreover, *DED* is divided into training (10000 images) and testing (1000 images) parts. The images for the training part are collected from *Kitti* (object part) [GLU12] and *ETH* (Setup 1) [Ess+08] datasets, in which the bounding boxes of objects are annotated in the left images. In order to compute the heights of objects in the real world, for each object bounding box, its corresponding is searched on the right image. Given an object bounding box, most pixels on the left image should

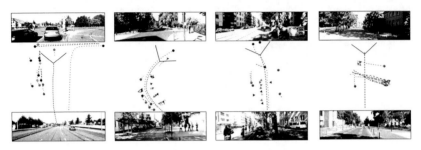

Figure 7.6: Examples of multiple object tracking and camera odometry on some sequences of the Kitti dataset. Each example (column) is represented by 3 rows: the first frame of the sequence (bottom), the last frame of the sequence (top), and in-between the extracted trajectories of all detected objects and the camera are represented by dashed lines, where the last observable positions are represented by circles (•) for cars, triangles (◄) for pedestrians and the V-shape for the camera. Each single object (a pedestrian or a car) is shown in a specific grey level.

match with their corresponding on the same epipolar line in the right image. Afterwards, the depth of the object is computed based on the position of its bounding boxes on the left and right images w.r.t camera parameters (i.e., focal length). Finally, the depth is used to compute the size (height and width) of the object in the real world. For the testing part, the images are collected from different sets *Kitti* (odometry) and *ETH* (Setup 2) datasets. In these datasets, object bounding boxes are not provided. Therefore, Deformable-Part-Model detector [Fel+10] is employed, where false positive detections are manually discarded. The ground truth of the testing part is computed in a similar way as the training part.

Kitti Tracking Dataset (KTD): For the evaluation of 3D trajectories extraction, the tracking dataset proposed by *Kitti* benchmark [GLU12] is used. The dataset consists of 21 sequences, where objects (e.g., cars and pedestrians) are tracked and represented by associated bounding-boxes over frames (only left images). In order to obtain the 3D position of a given object in the real world at each frame, the corresponding bounding box is projected from the image plan w.r.t camera parameters. For this, the depth is obtained by following the same steps as in *DED*. In this dataset, the ground truth of the camera odometry is not provided.

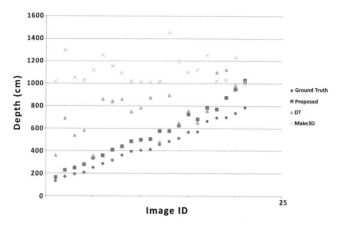

Figure 7.7: Depth estimation comparison between the proposed method (*Proposed*), *Ground Truth*, Depth Transfer method (*DT*), and *Make3D* method for 21 object examples.

7.2.2.2   Object-based Depth Estimation

For the evaluation of object-based depth estimation, *DED* dataset is employed. Given a query image (i.e., object bounding box), the size is first computed using the method described in Section 5.2. Later, the depth of the object is computed given the estimated focal length, the assumed camera height (Ʊ) and assumed pitch angle (β).

The evaluation of the proposed method is performed by comparing its output with those of two state-of-the-art depth estimation methods. Consequently, Depth Transfer proposed by Karsch *et al.* [KLK16] and Make3D proposed by Saxena *et al.* [SSN09] are employed in this comparison. Both methods estimate depth maps of images based on similar examples. Figure 7.7 illustrates 20 comparison examples of *Ground Truth* with estimated depths of the proposed method (*Proposed*), Depth transfer (*DT*) and *Make3D*. In this figure, the examples are sorted in ascending order according to their ground truth depths. As demonstrated in the comparison figure, contrary to the-state-of-the-art methods, *Proposed* estimates depths with a relative stable deviation to those of the ground truth. Furthermore, Figure 7.7 demonstrates that the depth error is proportional to the ground truth depth, where the farther the object, the higher the error. This can be explained by the impact of the focal length error, where farther objects are more influenced by the focal length error.

For a detailed evaluation, the obtained result of object-based depth estimation for the 1000 testing objects is presented in Figure 7.8. To verify the sensitivity of *Proposed*, the first 10 boxes in the figure denote its depth errors considering a different number of candidates

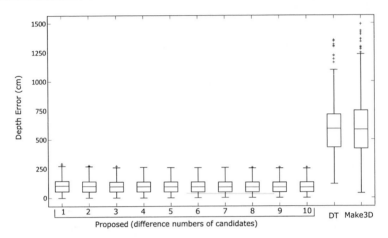

Figure 7.8: Overall comparison of the proposed method *Proposed*, Depth Transfer method (*DT*), and *Make3D* method, considering different numbers of candidates.

(from 1 to 10). The last two boxes represent the depth errors of *DT* and *Make3D*, respectively. As can be seen, *Proposed* provides the best result among the presented methods, where its average error does not exceed $1m$ regardless the number of candidates. Meanwhile, the depth errors in the two other methods are more than $5m$. Furthermore, the small deviation error of *Proposed* makes it suitable for tracking objects in the real world, where the depths of objects deviate with a relative stable error. Although this error deviation slightly increases for farther objects, it does not change the spatial relationship between objects. Additionally, *Proposed* is not sensitive to the number of candidates, where the obtained results considering one candidate and 10 candidates are almost similar. The reason of this is due to the small difference between the heights of objects in the same category, where the range of their heights is usually very narrow and limited.

The result presented in this part of the section demonstrates the effectiveness of the proposed method in estimating the heights of objects, and thus estimating their depths. Explicitly, the stable deviation of the depth error for all objects, which belong to the same scene, makes the method robust for 3D trajectory extraction. This is because the deviation does not considerably affect the relationships among objects, rather it disturbs the relation between the set of objects and the camera. It is crucial to note, the accuracy of the estimated depth is highly relevant to the estimated focal length.

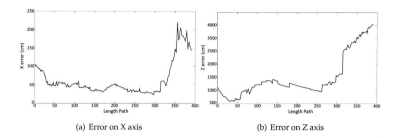

(a) Error on X axis   (b) Error on Z axis

Figure 7.9: Mean errors on X and Z axes at each appearance timestamp.

7.2.2.3 Trajectory Extraction

In this part, the overall evaluation of the 3D trajectory extraction method (Section 5) is presented and discussed. This experiment is conducted on *KTD*, where the estimated trajectories are compared to their corresponding in the ground truth. As already mentioned in the description of the dataset, the ground truth of camera odometry is not provided. Thus, only the position of an object w.r.t current camera position can be computed for the ground truth. On the other hand, the proposed method (*Proposed*) provides for each object its sequential positions w.r.t the initial position of the camera. Since it is not possible to prepare the 3D trajectories for the ground truth, all trajectories obtained by *Proposed* are transformed to independent positions w.r.t the camera. Given a 3D trajectory, the transformation of each position at time t is performed w.r.t the inverse camera position $(-R_t^\mathsf{T} \times T_t)$. With this transformation, a practical evaluation is ensured without losing any information. Due to this transformation, the adopted coordinate system for this evaluation always follows the camera coordinate system, whose centre is the optical centre of the camera and its axes are: X: lateral axis, Y: vertical axis and Z: longitudinal axis.

The main problem of extracting 3D trajectories of objects is the error accumulation, which may cause a large deviation after a certain time of tracking. Therefore, the overall mean errors (the difference between *Proposed* and the ground truth *cm*), on X and Z axes in terms of the appearance timestamps, are presented in Figure 7.9. Specifically, the tth mean error is computed for all objects in their t^{th} appearance timestamps. For this, the appearance timestamp of each object is set to 0 in its first appearance. The presented result in Figure 7.9 is obviously unstable, which indicates that the estimation error is independent for each appearance timestamps and does not accumulate over time. This can be explained by the movements of objects in different directions, where they may partially correct their positions over time.

Since the previous evaluation does not allow to analyse the obtained result concretely,

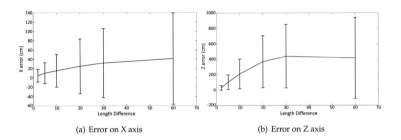

(a) Error on X axis   (b) Error on Z axis

Figure 7.10: Transition of the means and standard deviations of errors in stride estimation on X and Z axes for gaps of appearance timestamps (t_g= 2,10,20,30,60 frames).

another evaluation is carried out for more accurate analysis. Consequently, instead of computing the independent error at each appearance timestamps, the error here is calculated based on object stride estimation (direction and velocity). Given an object trajectory, the stride means the difference between its positions in two frames. The reason is that in 3D trajectory extraction, the correct starting point of the object's trajectory is not that important as the correct stride. Therefore, the strides of all pairs of appearance timestamps t_i and t_j, on X and Z axes, are computed for both *Proposed* and the ground truth. Afterwards, the errors are computed as the absolute difference between the computed strides of the proposed method and those of the ground truth. The mean and the standard deviation of different gaps of appearance timestamps t_g are presented in Figure 7.10. The presented result in the figure demonstrates that the errors slightly increase as the tracking time increases, which is caused by the error accumulation.

In addition to the tracking time, the ground truth depths of objects also influence the accuracy of the result. As discussed in the evaluation of object-based depth estimation, the depth error of an object is proportional to its actual depth. This also applies on the estimation of its transition in the real world over time. Therefore, it is important to assess the estimation of 3D trajectories based on the actual depths of their executors. For this, the mean and standard deviation error are presented in Figure 7.11 in terms of the ground truth depths of objects. The error values are computed on X and Z axes for all objects having the same ground truth depth = $10, 20, ..., 90m$. The result, illustrated in Figure 7.11, concludes that farther objects have higher errors than close ones. In other words, the inverse correlation between the motion of objects on the image plane and their distances to the camera negatively affects the accuracy of the trajectory estimation.

The above results validate the capability of *Proposed* to estimate the 3D positions of objects with a significant lack of information such as the intrinsic camera parameters and the depths

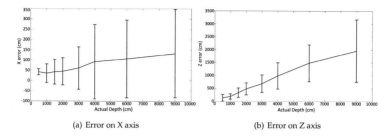

(a) Error on X axis   (b) Error on Z axis

Figure 7.11: Transition of means and standard deviations of errors on X and Z axes in terms of object's depth.

of objects. Despite the impact of the imprecise focal length and size in the extraction of the first position of an object, the proposed method can estimate the stride of the object with sufficient precision.

7.3 Camera Parameters Estimation

The aim of this section is to validate the sub-methods presented in Chapter 5, which focuses on estimating the intrinsic and extrinsic camera parameters. For intrinsic parameters, a detailed explanation about focal length estimation is given. Eventually, the estimation of the extrinsic parameters is assessed by a comprehensive experiment on a challenging dataset.

7.3.1 Focal Length Estimation

7.3.1.1 Datasets

Focal length Estimation Dataset (FED): This dataset is employed to evaluate the generality of focal length estimation. *FED* consists of two parts: training and testing parts, where the training part contains 75000 images randomly collected from *Mirflickr* [HTL10]. The images in this part cover a wide range of focal lengths ($[2.5, 550]mm$). Here, all images are defined with their corresponding semantic classes (among 23 predetermined classes: Animal, Natural view, Street, etc.). Moreover, each training image is associated with its EXIF, which encloses the important information of the acquisition, mainly the focal length (mm) and CCD width (mm). Similarly to the training part, the testing part is collected from *Mirflickr* containing 1000 images, each of which is associated with its EXIF. Here, the EXIFs are used to evaluate the focal length estimation. The images in both sets are carefully selected so that they do not intersect with each other. Furthermore, the variation in these

Table 7.5: Comparison between ground truth (GT) and estimated focal length(EFL) for the four query images

	Query 1	Query 2	Query 3	Query 4
GT (mm)	16.6	17	3.36	4.95
EFL (mm)	22	15	5.8	7.3

sets, in terms of semantic contents, focal lengths and used cameras, helps to examine the generality of the focal length estimation method.

Focal length Estimation Dataset* (FED*): The output of the focal length estimation method is used for certain subsequent methods, which are presented in Chapter 5. Therefore, for a concrete evaluation, another dataset called *FED**, which consists of 1000 images collected from *DED* (both training and test parts), is employed. The images of *FED** are practically from two visual domains: *Kitti* [GLU12] and *ETH* [Ess+08].

7.3.1.2   Evaluation

The validation of focal length estimation is performed on both datasets *FED* and *FED** in order to prove the effectiveness of the method. Depending on the explanation in Section 5.1, the focal length is computed in a pixel unit, after estimating the ratio of f_{mm} to the CCD width. It has to be noted that the focal length errors cannot be assessed on the basis of pixel unit [BSG17a]. Therefore, exclusively for this evaluation, the focal length is estimated in millimetre. However, for other experiments, in which the proposed method is used, the focal length is estimated exactly as in the description.

For qualitative analysis, Figure 7.12 illustrates four examples of query images, whose focal lengths are estimated using the proposed method. The two first examples are from *FED* dataset, where the two last one are from *FED** dataset. For each query image in Figure 7.12, the most similar candidates in terms of spatial characteristic are retrieved (line **a**). Besides, line **b** and line **c** represent the retrieved candidates based on semantic and blurry similarities, respectively. Moreover, Table 7.5 indicates the estimated and the ground truth focal lengths of the four examples. As demonstrated in the table, despite the large variety of focal lengths the estimated one is very close to the ground truth.

To quantitatively assess the proposed method, the error is computed as the absolute difference between the estimated and the ground truth focal lengths. For the evaluation on *FED** dataset, the overall mean error $\simeq 2.59mm$ and the overall deviation $\simeq 0.85mm$. This

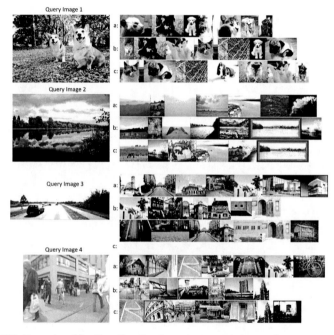

Figure 7.12: Examples of focal length estimation: given a query image, the seven most similar candidates in spatial characteristics (Line **a**), seven most similar candidates in semantic content (Line **b**) and seven most similar candidates in blurry degree (Line **c**) are retrieved.

small deviation error is due to the high similarity of images within the dataset, where they are practically from two visual domains. This is likely to lead to retrieving similar candidates for images of the same domain, and thus the estimated focal lengths are convergent. Statistically, the mean error in the first visual domain ($Kitti$) $\approx 2.69mm$, whereas the deviation $\approx 0.77mm$. For the second visual domain (ETH), the mean error $\approx 1.66mm$ and the deviation $\approx 1.08mm$.

Despite the fact that the images in the training and FED^* datasets are different, the obtained result is adequately accurate. This is due to the large-scale training dataset, which contains a considerable variety of images in terms of both semantic contents and focal length values. Consequently, the training dataset is most probably to enclose several similar candidates to test images. Furthermore, Equation 5.2 is supposed to neglect candidates with isolated focal lengths. Here, the proposed method adopts a focal length value in the range of most candidates. Additionally, the focal lengths in video recordings are supposed to be relatively lower than those of still images. This is to maintain the view stable while moving the camera. The focal length estimation can, therefore, be improved by retrieving only video frames as candidates. Due to the unavailability of such datasets, it is assumed in this work that the focal lengths of videos are in the range $[2.5, 100]mm$.

For more general evaluation, Figure 7.15 presents the error range histogram of focal lengths, which are estimated for FED dataset. Each bar in this histogram denotes the frequency difference between the estimated focal length (f_{mm}) and the ground truth ($\acute{f}_{mm}$) for a specific range. Figure 7.15 indicates that the focal lengths of about 40% of test images are estimated with errors less than $10mm$, and the errors for about 80% of test images are less than $30mm$ [BSG17a]. In addition, the mean estimation error on $FED \approx 29.03mm$, while the median error $\approx 13.74mm$.

To accurately estimate the focal length, it is crucial that most of the retrieved candidates have similar focal lengths. However, the wide range does not ensure this property. For this, Figure 7.13 examines the sensitivity of the proposed method in terms of the mean error considering different candidates' number. More specifically, 10 sets are randomly selected from the testing part of FED, where each set consists of 100 images. For each image, the focal length is estimated using a different number of candidates = $\{3, 4, \cdots, 15\}$. Afterwards, considering all images in all sets, the mean error for each number of candidates is computed. The errors demonstrated in Figure 7.13 vary from $29.5mm$ to $32.5mm$. This implies that the proposed method is not highly sensitive to the number of candidates, where the focal lengths of selected candidates are close. Furthermore, the mean error, with the consideration of seven candidates, $\approx 29.76mm$, which is very close to the smallest error.

Similarly to the number of candidates, a, b and c in Equation 5.2 are given parameters, and their manipulations can change the result. Accordingly, the same approach used for

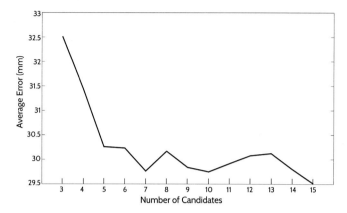

Figure 7.13: Average error of estimated focal lengths considering different candidates = $\{3, 4, \cdots, 15\}$.

analysing the sensitivity to the number of candidates is performed to obtain the result of different combinations of a, b and c. Figure 7.14 presents the mean errors considering 1000 combinations of parameters, where each parameter varies from 0.1 to 1.0 with a step size of 0.1. As demonstrated, the mean errors of all combinations are very narrow (it ranges from about 29.5 to 32.5mm). Particularly, the average error for the combination $a = 0.7, b = 0.9, c = 0.8$ is about 29.65mm.

The focal length is the most important factor to understand the relationship between the image plane the real world. Notably, its deviation has a high impact to the projection of objects into the real world. The map in Figure 7.16 illustrates the deviation of a computed depth considering a focal length error of 1mm. Since the values of the actual depth and focal length also have significant impacts to the depth deviation, the map is produced in terms of the actual focal length and actual depth. For a concrete example, a real focal length = 45mm with an estimated error 10mm yields to a depth deviation of 133.4cm in a case where the actual depth is 6m. This concludes that the depth deviation of a 10mm focal length error is reasonable compared to the ground truth depth.

Although the proposed method does not estimate focal lengths with high precision, the presented result validates its efficiency in estimating focal lengths with reasonable errors without any geometrical information. With this, the approximate focal length of any image can be estimated regardless its content contrary to existing methods. However, the estimated focal length cannot be relied upon for applications, which require very precise result.

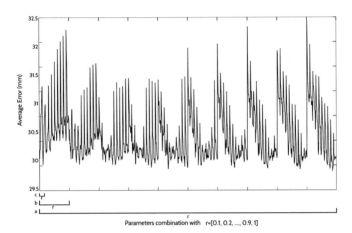

Figure 7.14: Average error of estimated focal lengths considering different parameters combination of a, b and c

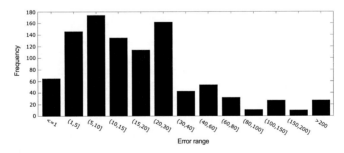

Figure 7.15: Error range histogram in focal length estimation.

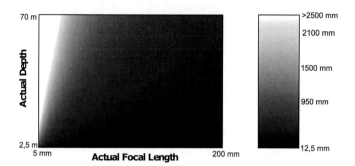

Figure 7.16: Depth difference map for $1mm$ focal length error.

7.3.2 Camera Odometry Estimation

7.3.2.1 Dataset

Kitti Odometry Dataset (KOD): For camera odometry, a challenging dataset is proposed by *Kitti* vision benchmark [GLU12]. This dataset consists of 11 stereo sequences (00-10) for training, each of which is acquired under different conditions to cover different scenarios (e.g., high street, rural and urban areas). The training part of *KOD* is prepared in such way that it is presented by left images, depth maps and segment maps. For testing, *Kitti* vision benchmark proposes another set that also consists of stereo sequences (11-21). However, the testing part of *KOD* considers only the left images of all sequences. The main challenge of this dataset lies in the velocity variation of the acquisition device (camera) between sequences, and also within the one sequence.

7.3.2.2 Evaluation

The aim of this section is to measure the ability of the proposed method "*Proposed*" to localise the camera over time, with the consideration of only monocular images. For this, *Proposed* described in Chapter 5 is performed on *KOD* dataset. Practically, the position of the camera at each timestamp t is computed based on the rotation matrices $R_{0:t}$ and translation vectors $T_{O:t}$ for all pairs of consecutive frames. This is considered as the combination of the accumulated rotation matrix $\mathcal{R}_t$ and the accumulated translation vector $\mathcal{T}_t$. All experimental analyses in this part are performed on the basis of $\mathcal{R}_t$ and $\mathcal{T}_t$. Moreover, to ensure the stability of the selection of candidates for segment-based depth estimation, the retrieved candidates can be highly weighted to be selected in successive frames. To concretely illustrate the output of

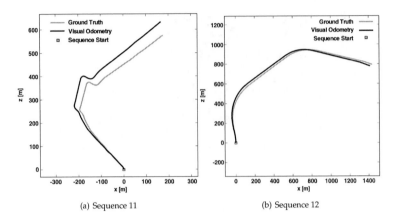

(a) Sequence 11   (b) Sequence 12

Figure 7.17: Examples of camera trajectories extracted by *Proposed* (dark) compared to the ground truth (bright).

Proposed, Figure 7.17 presents two examples of extracted camera trajectories compared to the ground truth. Despite the length of the path, the obtained trajectory is very close to the ground truth.

For an overall evaluation, Kitti benchmark [GLU12] provides a transparent evaluation system. Using the online system, the result obtained by *Proposed* is compared to the result of the state-of-the-art methods. The detailed comparison is accessed on the Kitti website[1], where *Proposed* is listed under the name *EB3DTE+RJMCM*. The comparison of 16 independent methods, which are listed on the Kitti website, is illustrated in Figure 7.18. Here, only the methods which focus on monocular-based visual odometry are considered. The methods are presented in ascending order from the lowest overall percentage error to the highest. Figure 7.18 distinguishes these methods by three different shades of grey, where *Proposed* is represented by black shade. The six methods in argent shade (brighter) are those which are identified with published papers and detailed descriptions. The remaining ones in silver shade (brightest) are completely anonymous, and therefore, they are not considered in the comparison analysis. For each method, the overall percentage error is computed for all possible sub-sequences of different lengths (5, 10, 50, 100,..., 400) [BSG17a]. As illustrated in the comparison figure, *Proposed* is in the middle position with a percentage error $\simeq 5.5\%$. Furthermore, the percentage error of the best method $\simeq 2.24\%$ and that of the worst $\simeq 20.95\%$. Although the result of *Proposed* does not reach those of the three first methods, the reliance

---

[1]http://www.cvlibs.net/datasets/kitti/eval_odometry.php

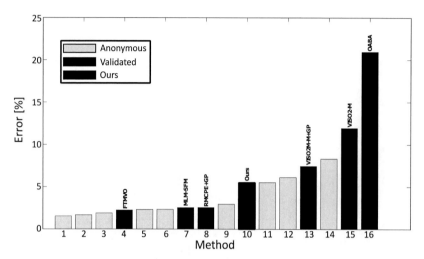

Figure 7.18: Evaluation of camera odometry on Kitti dataset (11 to 21 sequences) compared to other methods(FTMVO[MM15], MLM-SFM[SM14], RMCPE+GP[MM14], VISO2M-M+GP[SM14], VISO2-M[SM14], OABA[FKM16]).

on fewer assumptions makes the proposed method more robust in challenging conditions (i.e., a serious lack of information).

For more detailed analyses, The overall percentage errors of the translation and rotation are computed for all sequences with path lengths $t = k \cdot 100, k \in \{1, 2, \cdots, 8\}$. Consequently, the corresponding mean percentage errors are presented in Figure 7.19. In Figure 7.23(a), the slight upward trend, formed by the translation error, demonstrates that the error accumulates over time. Contrariwise, the rotation error decreases for longer path lengths as illustrated in Figure 7.23(b). This is mainly due to the specific characteristics of the used dataset, where the path in a sequence is more likely to be straight as it becomes longer.

To evaluate the performance of the proposed method in terms of the velocity of the camera, Figure 7.20 illustrates the corresponding translation and the rotation errors. For this purpose, the mean percentage errors of all sub-sequences in *KOD* are computed at each camera velocity $V = k \cdot 10, \quad k \in \{1, 2, \cdots, 9\}$. According to Figure 7.20, both the translation and rotation errors have non-monotonic trends. Therefore, the camera velocity cannot be considered as a predominant factor in the overall accuracy of camera localisation. However,

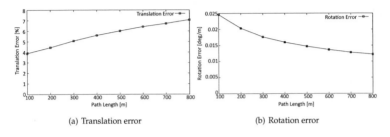

(a) Translation error   (b) Rotation error

Figure 7.19: Translation and rotation errors in terms of path length.

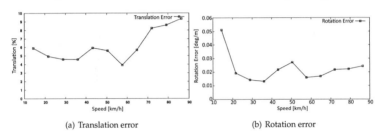

(a) Translation error   (b) Rotation error

Figure 7.20: Translation and rotation errors in terms of camera velocity

by analysing small ranges of the camera velocity and its error curve, it is concluded that the translation error increases with increasing velocity (highway: $> 70km/h$). The reason is that the change between consecutive frames in such a situation is very significant, and thus the accuracy of key-points matching decreases. On the contrary, the rotation error is low, due to the straightness of the path as the camera velocity is high. In low velocity scenarios, the translation error decreases as a result of the small movements of the camera. Unlike the translation, the error of the rotation increases, because the camera is supposed to turn in different directions in lower velocities. Also, Figure 7.20(b) proves this conclusion, where as shown, the highest rotation error is obtained in the lowest velocity.

The results presented and discussed in this section approve that the proposed method is capable of estimating the position of the camera over time. In addition, these results are obtained with relying neither on the existence of admitted feature points nor the intrinsic camera parameters, such as the focal length and the principal point. Furthermore, it is demonstrated in the above discussion that the proposed method is adapted to deal with sequences taken under different conditions, such as velocity difference, environment variation and path length.

7.4   Trajectory Analysis

This section focuses on evaluating two applications of trajectory analysis, whose methods are described in Chapter 6. First, the result of convoy detection is discussed. Second, the detection of suspicious activities in crowded scenes is evaluated.

7.4.1   Convoy Detection

7.4.1.1   Dataset

Convoy Detection Dataset (CDD): This experiment employs *ODD* dataset to evaluate key-points-based object detection, which is introduced in Section 7.1.1. The ground truth of convoys was manually prepared, where each group of pedestrians (two or more) is annotated from its beginning until its end.

7.4.1.2   Evaluation

Using *CDD* dataset, the proposed convoy detection *"Proposed"* is assessed, where the trajectories are obtained using the method described in Section 3.1. Before presenting statistical analysis, Figure 7.21 depicts an example of detected convoys from *CDD*. Here, the lines of the same grey level denote the trajectories of pedestrians that belong to one convoy, whereas the associated number denotes the convoy duration.

Furthermore, a detailed analysis of the proposed method on *CDD* is presented in Table 7.6. As mentioned above, the trajectories are obtained by performing the object detection method discussed in Section 3.1 and evaluated in Section 7.1.1. The adopted parameters of this method are those which provide the median result. Basically, the detected convoys are highly affected by the object detection step, which is likely to output false detections or miss true ones. Therefore, to demonstrate the effectiveness of the proposed method in a fair manner, three different cases are considered in this work. In the first case 'S1', the resulting convoys of the proposed method are compared to all convoys of the ground truth. For the second case 'S2', the result of *Proposed* is compared to a part of the ground truth. This part contains only convoys whose members are successfully detected by the proposed object detection method. To evaluate *Proposed* without the impact of falsely detected objects, the last case 'S3' is carried out by neglecting the detected convoys, which are formed by *false positive pedestrian detection (FPPD)*.

The result presented in Table 7.6 demonstrates that *Proposed* is capable of accurately detecting convoys. As given by the recall of 'S1', an important number of true positive

Figure 7.21: An example of convoy detection.

Table 7.6: Convoy detection result.

	S1	S2	S3
Recall	0.88	0.97	0.97
Precision	0.47	0.47	0.92

convoys are correctly detected. However, the precision indicates that among the detected convoys, a high number of them are false. This is mainly due to the false detected objects, where the proposed convoy detection method is very sensitive to the relevance of object detection. Furthermore, by neglecting the ground truth convoys, whose members failed to be detected by the method of object detection, the recall increases with about 9% as seen in 'S2'. The relatively small difference between the recalls of 'S1' and 'S2' implies that only a few true positive convoys are missed, which is desirable for security surveillance [Bou+16a]. By contrast, the precision of convoy detection significantly increases as the false detections are neglected. As indicated by the precision difference between 'S1' and 'S3', the precision of object detection heavily reflects on that of convoy detection. This is due to the double detection, where if one object is wrongly detected as two object, it is unmistakably considered as a convoy. In spite of this, the proposed convoy detection method provides highly accurate results, considering that all objects are correctly detected.

In group activity analysis, it is not only important to detect the existence of the event (e.g., convoy) but also its starting and ending times, in addition to its continuity. Therefore, the beginning and the end of each convoy (detected by *Proposed* and ground truth) is manually annotated. Afterwards, the frequency of cohesion is computed as the number of interruptions per convoy. Figure 7.22(a) displays the corresponding histogram, which signifies that more than 50% of detected convoys are not interrupted [Bou+16a]. Moreover, the number of interruptions in the remaining detected convoys is low compared to their lengths and with the consideration of the high crowd density. Notably, the longest convoy in the ground truth appears in 156 frames ($\simeq$ 1,8 minutes) [Bou+16a]. This result validates the cohesion of the convoys detected using the proposed method.

Additionally, another experiment is performed to evaluate the temporal coverage of the extracted convoys compared to their ground truth temporal existences. Figure 7.22(b) illustrates the histogram that expresses the frequency of convoy completeness. As depicted in the figure, 52 convoys ($\simeq$ 35%) among 148 annotated ones are completely detected and tracked for their entire existences. Moreover, about 96 of detected convoys ($\simeq$ 65%) are tracked for more than 80% of their existences. Since the ground truth was manually annotated, it is likely to contain uncertain convoys in terms of starting and ending times. Therefore, with a tolerance of 20% of incompleteness in the detected convoys, 65% of "complete" detection and tracking is reasonable.

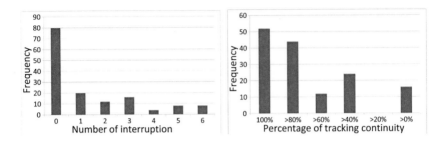

Figure 7.22: Left: interruption histogram (a), Right: tracking continuity histogram (b).

7.4.2   Suspicious Activity Detection

7.4.2.1   Dataset

Suspicious Activity Dataset (SAD): The dataset adopted for this task is collected from the pedestrian walking dataset [YLW15b], which is described earlier in Section 7.1.1. Among more than 12000 trajectories that are provided in [YLW15b], the first 3490 trajectories are considered. It has to be noted that the standards, which characterise activities into suspicious and normal, differ from one user to another. Therefore, the trajectories are manually annotated with the fact that this annotation admits some uncertainty. Consequently, 438 trajectories are regarded as suspicious, while the remaining ones are counted as normals.

7.4.2.2   Evaluation

To evaluate the method proposed for suspicious activity detection, *SAD* dataset is used. A set of 1000 trajectories is dedicated to training the classier. In addition, a set of 200 trajectories is selected to represent the pure normal examples, whose centroid is the positive seed (normal activity). The training set is clustered into 150 groups using *k-means*. Since the classifier is not trained with labelled negative examples (suspicious activities), the testing part contains all annotated trajectories. Figure 7.23 illustrates two examples of full normal and extreme suspicious activities, where a normal activity for this dataset is assumed to be stable over time to reach a precise destination.

For a general evaluation, the trajectories in both parts (training and testing) are admitted for their original durations. In simpler words, the trajectories do not have the same length. Therefore, their extracted features are re-sampled to have a specific length (10 for each characteristic). Table 7.7 presents the comparison between the proposed mehtod (*Proposed*)

(a) Absolute normal activity   (b) Extreme suspicious activity

Figure 7.23: Examples of normal and suspicious activities.

Table 7.7: A comparison between the proposed method (*Proposed*) and *k-means* clustering using low-level features. The classes *"Normal"* and *"Suspicious"* are denoted by (+) and (-), respectively.

	Precision (+)	Recall (+)	Precision (-)	Recall (-)	Precision (macro-average)	Recall (macro-average)
Proposed	**0.933**	**0.968**	**0.707**	**0.513**	**0.820**	**0.741**
k-means	0.877	0.913	0.153	0.106	0.515	0.509

and a simple *k-means* [Llo06] clustering on *SAD*, using the high-level features (codebook). Here, *k-means* is the baseline method, with the assumption that clustering data leads to the isolation of abnormal entities in the smallest cluster. Moreover, high-level features are those extracted using codebook approach, where 15 words are generated from each characteristic (Section 6.2). The result of the proposed method is computed as the average of 10 tests. In each of these tests, the training and the positive (seed) sets are randomly selected from the entire *SAD*.

The presented result demonstrates the effectiveness of *Proposed* compared to the baseline method. Concretely, given the experimental test with the average result, 265 suspicious activities among 438 are correctly detected, and only 147 normal activities among 3052 are detected as suspicious. However, a significant number of suspicious activities are miss-detected, which might be caused by the lengthiness of some trajectories. More precisely, the durations of the abnormality in several trajectories are very short compared to the total lengths, and thus a serious decline in the impact of anomalies. To overcome this, at each time t, the last activities in the trajectories (from $t-15$ to t) are independently considered. Specifically, for each trajectory in the data, all possible windows (sub-trajectories) of a length = 15 are extracted and reinitialised to 0. A trajectory is suspicious if at least one of its

Table 7.8: The result of *Proposed* on the extracted sub-trajectories.

	Precision (+)	Recall (+)	Precision (-)	Recall (-)	Precision (macro-average)	Recall (macro-average)
Proposed	0.953	0.963	0.724	0.671	0.839	0.817

sub-trajectories is detected as suspicious. Table 7.8 shows the results of *Proposed* on sub-trajectories.

The above results prove that the adoption of a specific length slightly improves the detection where, among 438 suspicious activities, 144 are miss-detected. This miss-detection is more likely to be due to the different durations of the abnormality in all trajectories. On the one hand, a long duration is a crucial factor in some abnormal activities. In this case, the division to sub-trajectories makes the abnormality fade. On the other hand, in some case, the abnormality is characterised by the short duration. Thus, without dividing long trajectories, the normality is prevailing.

The results presented in this section validates the effectiveness of combining codebook and PU approaches to detect suspicious activities without relying on concrete training examples. Precisely, among a large unlabelled data, only small number of normal activities has to be labelled to train a classifier for normal/suspicious activities.

Chapter 8

Conclusion

This chapter is dedicated to summarising the principal conclusions of the proposed framework and its modules, by collecting most essential findings, obtained during the evaluation of the present work. Furthermore, an insight into possible future directions is discussed for the purpose of improving and generalising the proposed methods.

8.1   Summary

Recently, trajectory analysis has been drawn to the attention of many research communities, due to its effectiveness to solve several open problems [Zhe15]. Since cameras are one of the most used devices nowadays, this dissertation addresses the problem of extracting 3D trajectories of objects from 2D videos in order to analyse human activities. In this respect, several novel methods are developed and introduced in a structured way, going through object detection, 3D trajectory extraction and trajectory-based activity analysis.

For object detection, two methods focusing on detecting pedestrians in crowded scenes are presented and evaluated. The first one is introduced in Section 3.1, where the idea is to consider an object as a set of key-points that are extracted from a still image. To improve the detection, the sequential positions of key-points in an image sequence are employed. To validate the effectiveness of the method, its result is evaluated and compared to the ground truth in Section 7.1.1. Moreover, it has been noticed that the detection is remarkably sensitive to the parameters, which have therefore to be tuned according to the characteristics of the video. Regarding the second method, Section 3.2 expounds the systematic way followed to search for possible candidates being more likely to contain objects. Sections. 7.1.2 shows the promising results of the proposed object detection method and the effectiveness of the combination of selective search and CNN-based feature extraction.

The problem of 3D trajectory extraction is discussed in this work by two approaches.

The first one considers moving objects in 2D surveillance videos. As described in Chapter 4, this approach combines object detection and depth estimation to initialise the first position of a given object. From that position, the particle filtering takes over the process of tracking the object in the real world. In Section 7.2.1, the efficiency of this combination is evaluated based on experimental tests. On the one hand, the capability of this approach in extracting 3D trajectories from 2D videos is demonstrated given a reasonable result. On the other hand, due to the unstable consistency of both depth estimation and object detection, the presented statistical analysis indicates the necessity of sophisticated cues to generalise the approach. Consequently, the second approach addresses the same problem from a more generic perspective. Chapter 5 introduces a complete sub-framework to extract 3D trajectories of objects from uncalibrated monocular moving videos. To compensate the lack of information related to camera parameters, the sub-framework starts with estimating the focal length of the camera. Despite the unavailability of known geometrical shapes, the obtained results are promising as indicated in Section 7.3.1. Arguably, the approximate focal length of any image can be estimated with the presented method, while other techniques fail. Moreover, the result presented in Section 7.2.2 validates the efficiency of the cue, on which the sub-framework relies to initialise the detected objects in the real world for their first appearances. The subsequent results in the same section substantiate that the enhancement of the particle filtering, in terms of variable state and sampling process, improves the tracking accuracy. Besides, the position of the camera over time is also estimated, by adopting an efficacious observation cue that relies on examples. The corresponding results are depicted in Section 7.3.2, which affirm that the camera is well localised in the real world without relying on admitted landmarks.

In order to investigate the discriminative ability of trajectory-based features in activity analysis, this dissertation presents two example applications in Chapter 6. In the first one, groups of people are detected considering their travelling time, separation time and relative distances. The experimental tests, discussed in Section 7.4.1, demonstrates the effectiveness of the detection method and the notable robustness of trajectories to detect convoys in crowded scenes. The second application deals specifically with the problem of detecting suspicious activities in crowded environments based on people's trajectories. As shown in Section 7.4.2, the proposed method achieves high detection accuracy, and hence supports the previous finding of the impressive discriminative power of trajectories in activity analysis.

In conclusion, the results, obtained on challenging datasets, indicate the high potential for solving current open problems in computer vision and multimedia. More precisely, each proposed method addresses a serious problem that has drawn researchers' attention. Moreover, more complex problems are targeted in this dissertation by combining two or more methods. Overall, the underlying dissertation proposed a structured scheme to accurately extract 3D trajectories of objects from uncalibrated monocular moving videos.

8.2 Future Work

During the implementation and the evaluation of the proposed methods, several parts were planned to be improved. Despite the satisfactory accuracy of the obtained results, improvements are possible to generalise the system and make it robust for more difficult scenarios. Basically, three points are considered to be the improvement keys in the planned future work, notably, the computation time, the result accuracy and the generality.

In order to improve the detection method, it is important to search for objects with a lower time cost. One possible way is to use GPU for the extraction of time-consuming features from images, such as HOG. To increase the detection accuracy, combining different CNN models can play an important role to classify the region candidates. The reason here is that every model is characterised with its specific discriminative strengthens. Additionally, instead of extracting candidates by merging small regions until completing the whole image, the inverse strategy is planned, with the aim to extract more reliable candidates. For this, the image is iteratively divided based on the non-continuity in its local characteristics. Another positive consequence of this strategy is reducing the computational time, where the division process does not necessarily reach the last step.

For the estimation of focal length and depths of objects, the large training datasets make them impractical for devices with low resources such as smartphones. Therefore, replacing these datasets with CNN-based models would allow them not only to run faster but also to reduce the hardware requirements. Here, it is assumed that a model built from a large scale dataset increases the accuracy of the estimation. Moreover, searching for known geometrical shape in the image is also intended to assist the focal length estimation.

The extraction of 3D trajectories is another essential phase in this work, which can be improved. To this end, an interesting extension is to consider the pose of objects with the aim of enhancing the prediction of their movements. Explicitly, the rotations of objects are not observable in the presented approach, despite its ability to precisely track these objects in the real world. Therefore, it is supposed that the estimation of objects' poses will help to track them in scenarios of more perturbed movements. As next step, a higher-level analysis of object interaction is possible, by introducing new models controlling their movements.

For the purpose of developing the estimation of camera odometry, there are different potential future directions. On the one hand, similarly to the focal length, the training dataset can be replaced with a CNN-based model, intending to speed up the process of depth estimation. On the other hand, the technique itself admits an important improvement to increase the accuracy. More specifically, the adoption of additional cues, such as the horizontal line, is important to stabilise the localisation of the camera over time. Furthermore, the poses of tracked objects can be involved to decrease the estimation error of the camera rotation.

Finally, the most important extension of this work will be dedicated to the development of new trajectory mining techniques. The motivation of this dissertation is to extract objects trajectories for activity analysis. Therefore, the next step is the detection of more complicated activity patterns by studying objects trajectories. For this purpose, discriminative features, especially CNN-based, are planned to be extracted from those trajectories. Considering an object activity, its detection can be combined with the tracking process towards building a feedback mechanism. Here, the intention is that the output of each process is used as a cue of the other one.

Abbreviations

2D	two dimensional vii, ix, x, 4–7, 16, 29, 30, 39, 43, 47, 106
3D	three dimensional vii, ix, x, 3, 4, 6, 7, 11, 13, 14, 16, 29, 30, 32, 33, 38–40, 47–49, 51, 54, 57, 59, 78, 79, 83, 84, 86–88, 105–107, 113
CCD	Charge-Coupled Device 43, 45, 89, 90
CDD	Convoy Detection Dataset 99
CNN	Convolutional Neural Network 25–27, 105, 107, 108, 113
DED	Depth Estimation Dataset 83–85, 90
EM	Expectation-Maximisation 12
EXIF	Exchangeable Image File Format 44, 89
FAST	Features from Accelerated Segment Test 22, 23
FED	Focal length Estimation Dataset 89, 90, 92
FED*	Focal length Estimation Dataset* 90, 92
FOV	Field-Of-View 43
fps	frames per second 13, 78
GPS	Global Positioning System 3
GPU	Graphics Processing Unit 16, 107
HOG	Histograms of Oriented Gradients 2, 10, 13, 107
KLT	Kanade-Lucas-Tomasi 48
KOD	Kitti Odometry Dataset 95, 97
KTD	Kitti Tracking Dataset 84, 87
MAP	Maximum A Posteriori 40, 42
MRF	Markov Random Field 14, 53

MS	Mean Shift 12
ODD	Object Detection Dataset 73, 74, 99
ODD*	Object Detection Dataset* 75
PU	Positive Unlabelled 66, 71, 104
RANSAC	RANdom SAmple Consensus 17, 46
RGB	Red-Green-Blue 9, 13, 26, 48, 78
RGB-D	Red-Green-Blue Depth 13, 16
RJ-MCMC	Reversible Jump Markov Chain Monte Carlo 6, 7, 14, 39, 42, 43, 59, 113, 119
ROI	Region-Of-Interest 22, 23
SAD	Suspicious Activity Dataset 102, 103
SIFT	Scale-Invariant Feature Transform 2, 23, 24, 35, 36, 38, 46, 49, 82
SVM	Support Vector Machine 10, 26, 44, 66, 68, 70
TED	Trajectory Extraction Dataset 78, 79, 82, 117

Notation Summary

List of Figures

List of Tables

List of Algorithms

Bibliography

[ADF12]   B. Alexe, T. Deselaers, and V. Ferrari. "Measuring the Objectness of Image Windows". In: *Pattern Analysis and Machine Intelligence (TPAMI), IEEE Transactions on* 34.11 (2012), pp. 2189–2202.

[AR11]   J.K. Aggarwal and M.S. Ryoo. "Human Activity Analysis: A Review". In: *ACM Computing Surveys (CSUR)* 43.3 (2011), pp. 1–43.

[Aru+02]   M.S. Arulampalam, S. Maskell, N. Gordon, and T. Clapp. "A tutorial on particle filters for online nonlinear/non-Gaussian Bayesian tracking". In: *Signal Processing, IEEE Transactions on* 50.2 (2002), pp. 174–188.

[AT11]   M. R. Amer and S. Todorovic. "A chains model for localizing participants of group activities in videos". In: *Computer Vision (ICCV), IEEE International Conference on*. 2011, pp. 786–793.

[Bao+12]   C. Bao, Y. Wu, H. Ling, and H. Ji. "Real time robust L1 tracker using accelerated proximal gradient approach". In: *Computer Vision and Pattern Recognition (CVPR), IEEE Conference on Computer*. 2012, pp. 1830–1837.

[Bas01]   T. Basar. "A New Approach to Linear Filtering and Prediction Problems". In: *Control Theory:Twenty-Five Seminal Papers (1932-1981)*. 2001, pp. 167–179.

[BCC13]   P. V. K. Borges, N. Conci, and A. Cavallaro. "Video-Based Human Behavior Understanding: A Survey". In: *Circuits and Systems for Video Technology (TCSVT), IEEE Transactions on* 23.11 (2013), pp. 1993–2008.

[BW16]   M. Buczko and V. Willert. "How to Distinguish Inliers from Outliers in Visual Odometry for High-speed Automotive Applications". In: *IEEE Intelligent Vehicles Symposium (IV)*. 2016, pp. 478–483.

[Can86]   J. Canny. "A Computational Approach to Edge Detection". In: *Pattern Analysis and Machine Intelligence (TPAMI), IEEE Transactions on* 8.6 (1986), pp. 679–698.

[CKG11]   M. C. Chang, N. Krahnstoever, and W. Ge. "Probabilistic group-level motion analysis and scenario recognition". In: *Computer Vision (ICCV), IEEE International Conference on*. 2011, pp. 747–754.

[Cos+17]   S. Cosar, G. Donatiello, V. Bogorny, C. Garate, L. O. Alvares, and F. Bremond. "Towards Abnormal Trajectory and Event Detection in Video Surveillance". In: *Circuits and Systems for Video Technology (TCSVT), IEEE Transactions on* 27.3 (2017), pp. 683–695.

[CP15]   I. Cvišić and I. Petrović. "Stereo odometry based on careful feature selection and tracking". In: *Mobile Robots (ECMR), European Conference on*. 2015, pp. 1–6.

[CPS13]   W. Choi, C. Pantofaru, and S. Savarese. "A General Framework for Tracking Multiple People from a Moving Camera". In: *Pattern Analysis and Machine Intelligence (TPAMI), IEEE Transactions on* 35.7 (2013), pp. 1577–1591.

[Cro+08]   P.A. Crook, V. Kellokumpu, G. Zhao, and M. Pietikainen. "Human Activity Recognition Using a Dynamic Texture Based Method". In: *British Machine Vision Conference (BMVC)*. 2008, pp. 1–10.

[CS10a]   J. Carreira and C. Sminchisescu. "Constrained parametric min-cuts for automatic object segmentation". In: *Computer Vision and Pattern Recognition (CVPR), IEEE Conference on Computer*. 2010, pp. 3241–3248.

[CS10b]   W. Choi and S. Savarese. "Multiple Target Tracking in World Coordinate with Single, Minimally Calibrated Camera". In: *Computer Vision (ECCV), European Conference on*. 2010, pp. 553–567.

[CV95]   C. Cortes and V. Vapnik. "Support-Vector Networks". In: *Machine Learning* 20.3 (1995), pp. 273–297.

[CWL15]   L. Cao, C. Wang, and J. Li. "Robust depth-based object tracking from a moving binocular camera". In: *Signal Processing* 112 (2015), pp. 154–161.

[Dai+08]   P. Dai, H. Di, L. Dong, L. Tao, and G. Xu. "Group Interaction Analysis in Dynamic Context". In: *Systems, Man, and Cybernetics, Part B (Cybernetics), IEEE Transactions on* 38.1 (2008), pp. 275–282.

[DH72]   R. O. Duda and P. E. Hart. "Use of the Hough Transformation to Detect Lines and Curves in Pictures". In: *Communications of the ACM* 15.1 (1972), pp. 11–15.

[DLR77]   A. P. Dempster, N. M. Laird, and D. B. Rubin. "Maximum likelihood from incomplete data via the EM algorithm". In: *Journal of The Royal Statistical Society, Series B* 39.1 (1977), pp. 1–38.

[Dol+05]   P. Dollar, V. Rabaud, G. Cottrell, and S. Belongie. "Behavior recognition via sparse spatio-temporal features". In: *Visual Surveillance and Performance Evaluation of Tracking and Surveillance, IEEE International Workshop on*. 2005, pp. 65–72.

[DT05]   N. Dalal and B. Triggs. "Histograms of oriented gradients for human detection". In: *Computer Vision and Pattern Recognition (CVPR), IEEE Conference on Computer*. 2005, pp. 886–893.

[EH14]   I. Endres and D. Hoiem. "Category-Independent Object Proposals with Diverse Ranking". In: *Pattern Analysis and Machine Intelligence (TPAMI), IEEE Transactions on* 36.2 (2014), pp. 222–234.

[ESC13]   J. Engel, J. Sturm, and D. Cremers. "Semi-dense Visual Odometry for a Monocular Camera". In: *Computer Vision (ICCV), IEEE International Conference on*. 2013, pp. 1449–1456.

[Ess+08]   A. Ess, B. Leibe, K. Schindler, and L. van Gool. "A Mobile Vision System for Robust Multi-Person Tracking". In: *Computer Vision and Pattern Recognition (CVPR), IEEE Conference on*. 2008, pp. 1–8.

[Ess+09]   A. Ess, B. Leibe, K. Schindler, and L. Van Gool. "Robust Multiperson Tracking from a Mobile Platform". In: *Pattern Analysis and Machine Intelligence (TPAMI), IEEE Transactions on* 31.10 (2009), pp. 1831–1846.

[Est+96]   M. Ester, H.-P. Kriegel, J. Sander, and X. Xu. "A density-based algorithm for discovering clusters in large spatial databases with noise." In: *Knowledge Discovery and Data Mining (KDD), ACM SIGKDD International Conference on*. 1996, pp. 226–231.

[Fel+10]   P. F. Felzenszwalb, R. B. Girshick, D. McAllester, and D. Ramanan. "Object Detection with Discriminatively Trained Part-Based Models". In: *Pattern Analysis and Machine Intelligence (TPAMI), IEEE Transactions on* 32.9 (2010), pp. 1627–1645.

[FKM16]   D. P. Frost, O. Kähler, and D. W. Murray. "Object-Aware Bundle Adjustment for Correcting Monocular Scale Drift". In: *Robotics and Automation (ICRA), IEEE International Conference on*. 2016, pp. 4770–4776.

[GA+12]   D. Gowsikhaa, S. Abirami, et al. "Suspicious Human Activity Detection from Surveillance Videos." In: *International Journal on Internet & Distributed Computing Systems* 2.2 (2012).

[Gar+13]   J. Garcia, A Gardel, I Bravo, J.L. Lazaro, and M. Martinez. "Tracking People Motion Based on Extended Condensation Algorithm". In: *Systems, Man, and Cybernetics: Systems, IEEE Transactions on* 43.3 (2013), pp. 606–618.

[GCR12]   W. Ge, R. T. Collins, and R. B. Ruback. "Vision-Based Analysis of Small Groups in Pedestrian Crowds". In: *Pattern Analysis and Machine Intelligence (TPAMI), IEEE Transactions on* 34.5 (2012), pp. 1003–1016.

[GFH16]   N. B. Ghrab, E. Fendri, and M. Hammami. "Abnormal Events Detection Based on Trajectory Clustering". In: *Computer Graphics, Imaging and Visualization (CGiV), International Conference on*. 2016, pp. 301–306.

[GGMCG15]   D. Gutierrez-Gomez, W. Mayol-Cuevas, and J.J. Guerrero. "Inverse depth for accurate photometric and geometric error minimisation in RGB-D dense visual odometry". In: *Robotics and Automation (ICRA), IEEE International Conference on*. 2015, pp. 83–89.

[GLU12]   A. Geiger, P. Lenz, and R. Urtasun. "Are we ready for Autonomous Driving? The KITTI Vision Benchmark Suite". In: *Computer Vision and Pattern Recognition (CVPR), IEEE Conference on*. 2012, pp. 3354–3361.

[GS12]   C. Chandrasekar G.T. Shrivakshan. "A Comparison of various Edge Detection Techniques used in Image Processing". In: *International Journal of Computer Science* 9.5-1 (2012), pp. 1694–0814.

[GS15]   V. K. Gnanavel and A. Srinivasan. "Abnormal Event Detection in Crowded Video Scenes". In: *Frontiers of Intelligent Computing: Theory and Applications (FICTA), International Conference on*. 2015, pp. 441–448.

[GSS93]   N. J. Gordon, D. J. Salmond, and A. F. M. Smith. "Novel approach to nonlinear/non-Gaussian Bayesian state estimation". In: *Radar and Signal Processing, IEE Proceedings F* 140.2 (1993), pp. 107–113.

[Gu+09]   C. Gu, J. J. Lim, P. Arbelaez, and J. Malik. "Recognition using regions". In: *Computer Vision and Pattern Recognition (CVPR), IEEE Conference on Computer*. 2009, pp. 1030–1037.

[GZS11]   A. Geiger, J. Ziegler, and C. Stiller. "StereoScan: Dense 3d Reconstruction in Real-time". In: *Intelligent Vehicles, IEEE Symposium on*. 2011, pp. 963–968.

[Han+14]   A. Handa, T. Whelan, J. McDonald, and A.J. Davison. "A benchmark for RGB-D visual odometry, 3D reconstruction and SLAM". In: *Robotics and Automation (ICRA), IEEE International Conference on*. 2014, pp. 1524–1531.

[Has70]   W. K. Hastings. "Monte Carlo Sampling Methods Using Markov Chains and Their Applications". In: *Biometrika* 57.1 (1970), pp. 97–109.

[Heb+13]   M. Heber, M. Godec, M. Rüther, P. M. Roth, and H. Bischof. "Segmentation-based tracking by support fusion". In: *Computer Vision and Image Understanding* 117.6 (2013), pp. 573–586.

[HEH08]   D. Hoiem, A. A. Efros, and M. Hebert. "Putting Objects in Perspective". In: *International Journal of Computer Vision (IJCV)* 80.1 (2008), pp. 3–15.

[HJS09]   H. Harzallah, F. Jurie, and C. Schmid. "Combining efficient object localization and image classification". In: *Computer Vision (ICCV), IEEE International Conference on*. 2009, pp. 237–244.

[HTL10]   M. J. Huiskes, B. Thomee, and M. S. Lew. "New Trends and Ideas in Visual Concept Detection: The MIR Flickr Retrieval Evaluation Initiative". In: *Multimedia Information Retrieval, International Conference on*. 2010, pp. 527–536.

[HZ04]   R. I. Hartley and A. Zisserman. *Multiple View Geometry in Computer Vision*. Second. Cambridge University Press, ISBN: 0521540518, 2004.

[HZD13]   Y. Hu, Y. Zhang, and L. S. Davis. "Unsupervised Abnormal Crowd Activity Detection Using Semiparametric Scan Statistic". In: *Computer Vision and Pattern Recognition Workshops, IEEE Conference on*. 2013, pp. 767–774.

[IB98]   M. Isard and A. Blake. "CONDENSATION—Conditional Density Propagation for Visual Tracking". In: *International Journal of Computer Vision (IJCV)* 29.1 (1998), pp. 5–28.

[Jeu+08]   H. Jeung, Man L. Yiu, X. Zhou, C. S Jensen, and H. T. Shen. "Discovery of convoys in trajectory databases". In: *Proceedings of the VLDB Endowment* 1.1 (2008), pp. 1068–1080.

[JF10]   K. Junghyun and C. P. Frank. "Visual Tracking via Particle Filtering on the Affine Group". In: *The International Journal of Robotics Research* 29.2-3 (2010), pp. 198–217.

[JFEM01]   A. D. Jepson, D. J. Fleet, and T. R. El-Maraghi. "Robust online appearance models for visual tracking". In: *Computer Vision and Pattern Recognition (CVPR), IEEE Conference on Computer*. Vol. 1. 2001, pp. 415–422.

[JGJ15]   M. Jaimez and J. Gonzalez-Jimenez. "Fast Visual Odometry for 3-D Range Sensors". In: *Robotics, IEEE Transactions on* 31.4 (2015), pp. 809–822.

[Jia+14]   Y. Jia, E. Shelhamer, J. Donahue, S. Karayev, J. Long, R. Girshick, S. Guadarrama, and T. Darrell. "Caffe: Convolutional Architecture for Fast Feature Embedding". In: *Multimedia (ACMMM), ACM International Conference on*. 2014, pp. 675–678.

[JML14]   O.H. Jafari, D. Mitzel, and B. Leibe. "Real-time RGB-D based people detection and tracking for mobile robots and head-worn cameras". In: *Robotics and Automation (ICRA), IEEE International Conference on*. 2014, pp. 5636–5643.

[JSZ08]   H. Jeung, H. Tao Shen, and X. Zhou. "Convoy queries in spatio-temporal databases". In: *Data Engineering (ICDE), IEEE International Conference on*. 2008, pp. 1457–1459.

[JU04]   S. J. Julier and J. K. Uhlmann. "Unscented filtering and nonlinear estimation". In: *Proceedings of the IEEE* 92.3 (2004), pp. 401–422.

[Kat02]   M. Katz. *Introduction to Geometrical Optics*. 2002.

[KBD05]   Z. Khan, T. Balch, and F. Dellaert. "MCMC-based particle filtering for tracking a variable number of interacting targets". In: *Pattern Analysis and Machine Intelligence (TPAMI), IEEE Transactions on* 27.11 (2005), pp. 1805–1819.

[KLK14]   K. Karsch, C. Liu, and S. B. Kang. "Depth Transfer: Depth Extraction from Video Using Non-Parametric Sampling". In: *Pattern Analysis and Machine Intelligence (TPAMI), IEEE Transactions on* 36.11 (2014), pp. 2144–2158.

[KLK16]   K. Karsch, C. Liu, and S. B. Kang. "Dense Image Correspondences for Computer Vision". In: 2016. Chap. Depth Transfer: Depth Extraction from Videos Using Nonparametric Sampling, pp. 173–205.

[KN09]   L. Kratz and K. Nishino. "Anomaly detection in extremely crowded scenes using spatio-temporal motion pattern models". In: *Computer Vision and Pattern Recognition (CVPR), IEEE Conference on*. 2009, pp. 1446–1453.

[KS13]   H. Koppula and A. Saxena. "Learning Spatio-Temporal Structure from RGB-D Videos for Human Activity Detection and Anticipation". In: *Machine Learning, International Conference on*. Vol. 28. 3. 2013, pp. 792–800.

[KSC13]   C. Kerl, J. Sturm, and D. Cremers. "Robust odometry estimation for RGB-D cameras". In: *Robotics and Automation (ICRA), IEEE International Conference on*. 2013, pp. 3748–3754.

[KSS07]   R. Kanai, B. R. Sheth, and S. Shimojo. "Dynamical evolution of motion perception". In: *Vision Research* 47.7 (2007), pp. 937–945.

[Kwo+14]   J. Kwon, H. S. Lee, F. C. Park, and K. M. Lee. "A Geometric Particle Filter for Template-Based Visual Tracking". In: *Pattern Analysis and Machine Intelligence (TPAMI), IEEE Transactions on* 36.4 (2014), pp. 625–643.

[Lan+12]   T. Lan, Y. Wang, W. Yang, S. N. Robinovitch, and G. Mori. "Discriminative Latent Models for Recognizing Contextual Group Activities". In: *Pattern Analysis and Machine Intelligence (TPAMI), IEEE Transactions on* 34.8 (2012), pp. 1549–1562.

[LBH09]   C. H. Lampert, M. B. Blaschko, and T. Hofmann. "Efficient Subwindow Search: A Branch and Bound Framework for Object Localization". In: *Pattern Analysis and Machine Intelligence (TPAMI), IEEE Transactions on* 31.12 (2009), pp. 2129–2142.

[Lee+05]   K.-C. Lee, J. Ho, M.-H. Yang, and D. Kriegman. "Visual Tracking and Recognition Using Probabilistic Appearance Manifolds". In: *Computer Vision and Image Understanding* 99.3 (2005), pp. 303–331.

[Lee+15]   D. G. Lee, H. I. Suk, S. K. Park, and S. W. Lee. "Motion Influence Map for Unusual Human Activity Detection and Localization in Crowded Scenes". In: *Circuits and Systems for Video Technology (TCSVT), IEEE Transactions on* 25.10 (2015), pp. 1612–1623.

[Li+12]   M. Li, T. Tan, W. Chen, and K. Huang. "Efficient Object Tracking by Incremental Self-Tuning Particle Filtering on the Affine Group". In: *Image Processing, IEEE Transactions on* 21.3 (2012), pp. 1298–1313.

[Li+15]   T. Li, H. Chang, M. Wang, B. Ni, R. Hong, and S. Yan. "Crowded Scene Analysis: A Survey". In: *Circuits and Systems for Video Technology (TCSVT), IEEE Transactions on* 25.3 (2015), pp. 367–386.

[LLJ08]   R. Liu, Z. Li, and J. Jia. "Image partial blur detection and classification". In: *Computer Vision and Pattern Recognition (CVPR), IEEE Conference on*. 2008, pp. 1–8.

[Llo06]   S. Lloyd. "Least Squares Quantization in PCM". In: *Information Theory, IEEE Transactions on* 28.2 (2006), pp. 129–137.

[Low99]   D.G. Lowe. "Object recognition from local scale-invariant features". In: *Computer Vision (ICCV), IEEE International Conference on*. Vol. 2. 1999, pp. 1150–1157.

[LSL14]   D. G. Lee, H. I. Suk, and S. W. Lee. "Modeling crowd motions for abnormal activity detection". In: *Advanced Video and Signal Based Surveillance (AVSS), IEEE International Conference on*. 2014, pp. 325–330.

[LYT11]   C. Liu, J. Yuen, and A. Torralba. "SIFT Flow: Dense Correspondence across Scenes and Its Applications". In: *Pattern Analysis and Machine Intelligence (TPAMI), IEEE Transactions on* 33.5 (2011), pp. 978–994.

[Mah+10]   V. Mahadevan, W. Li, V. Bhalodia, and N. Vasconcelos. "Anomaly detection in crowded scenes". In: *Computer Vision and Pattern Recognition (CVPR), IEEE Conference on*. 2010, pp. 1975–1981.

[MBM08]   S. Maji, A. C. Berg, and J. Malik. "Classification using intersection kernel support vector machines is efficient". In: *Computer Vision and Pattern Recognition (CVPR), IEEE Conference on Computer*. 2008, pp. 1–8.

[Men+15]   L. Meng, C. Zemin, W. Chuliang, and T. Ye. "A Survey of Video Object Tracking". In: *International Journal of Control and Automation* 8.9 (2015), pp. 303–312.

[MM14]   M. H. Mirabdollah and B. Mertsching. "On the Second Order Statistics of Essential Matrix Elements". In: *Pattern Recognition (GCPR), German Conference on.* 2014, pp. 547–557.

[MM15]   H. Mirabdollah and B. Mertsching. "Fast Techniques for Monocular Visual Odometry". In: *Pattern Recognition (GCPR), German Conference on.* 2015, pp. 297–307.

[Mor+14]   E. Morais, A. Ferreira, S. A. Cunha, R. M.L. Barros, A. Rocha, and S. Goldenstein. "A multiple camera methodology for automatic localization and tracking of futsal players". In: *Pattern Recognition Letters* (2014), pp. 21–30.

[MOS09]   R. Mehran, A. Oyama, and M. Shah. "Abnormal crowd behavior detection using social force model". In: *Computer Vision and Pattern Recognition (CVPR), IEEE Conference on.* 2009, pp. 935–942.

[Mou+10]   M. Moussaid, N. Perozo, S. Garnier, D. Helbing, and G. Theraulaz. "The Walking Behaviour of Pedestrian Social Groups and Its Impact on Crowd Dynamics". In: *PLoS ONE* 5.4 (2010), pp. 1–7.

[MS83]   R. J. Meinhold and N. D. Singpurwalla. "Understanding the Kalman Filter". In: *The American Statistician* 37.2 (1983), pp. 123–127.

[MT08]   B. T. Morris and M. M. Trivedi. "A Survey of Vision-Based Trajectory Learning and Analysis for Surveillance". In: *Circuits and Systems for Video Technology (TCSVT), IEEE Transactions on* 18.8 (2008), pp. 1114–1127.

[MT11]   B. T. Morris and M. M. Trivedi. "Trajectory Learning for Activity Understanding: Unsupervised, Multilevel, and Long-Term Adaptive Approach". In: *Pattern Analysis and Machine Intelligence (TPAMI), IEEE Transactions on* 33.11 (2011), pp. 2287–2301.

[Nar+15]   L. Nardi, B. Bodin, M. Z. Zia, J. Mawer, A. Nisbet, P. H. J. Kelly, A. J. Davison, M. Luján, M. F. P. O'Boyle, G. Riley, N. Topham, and S. Furber. "Introducing SLAMBench, a performance and accuracy benchmarking methodology for SLAM". In: *Robotics and Automation (ICRA), IEEE International Conference on.* 2015, pp. 5783–5790.

[NLN11]   M. N. Nguyen, X. Li, and S.-K. Ng. "Positive Unlabeled Learning for Time Series Classification". In: *Artificial Intelligence V2, International Joint Conference on.* 2011, pp. 1421–1426.

[Nor04]   A. E. Nordsjo. "A constrained extended Kalman filter for target tracking". In: *IEEE Radar Conference.* 2004, pp. 123–127.

[OT01]   A. Oliva and A. Torralba. "Modeling the Shape of the Scene: A Holistic Representation of the Spatial Envelope". In: *International Journal of Computer Vision (IJCV)* 42.3 (2001), pp. 145–175.

[Per+15]   M. Persson, T. Piccini, R. Mester, and M. Felsberg. "Robust Stereo Vi-
                sual Odometry from Monocular Techniques". In: *IEEE Intelligent Vehicles
                Symposium*. 2015, pp. 686–691.

[PMF08]   C. Piciarelli, C. Micheloni, and G. L. Foresti. "Trajectory-Based Anomalous
                Event Detection". In: *Circuits and Systems for Video Technology (TCSVT)*,
                IEEE Transactions on 18.11 (2008), pp. 1544–1554.

[PSACMN13]   A. Penate-Sanchez, J. Andrade-Cetto, and F. Moreno-Noguer. "Exhaustive
                Linearization for Robust Camera Pose and Focal Length Estimation". In:
                Pattern Analysis and Machine Intelligence (TPAMI), IEEE Transactions on
                35.10 (2013), pp. 2387–2400.

[RA09]   M. S. Ryoo and J. K. Aggarwal. "Semantic Representation and Recognition
                of Continued and Recursive Human Activities". In: *International Journal of
                Computer Vision (IJCV)* 82.1 (2009), pp. 1–24. ISSN: 0920-5691.

[RD06]   E. Rosten and T. Drummond. "Machine Learning for High-Speed Cor-
                ner Detection". In: *Computer Vision (ECCV), European Conference on*. 2006,
                pp. 430–443.

[Roh+16]   M. Rohrbach, A. Rohrbach, M. Regneri, S. Amin, M. Andriluka, M. Pinkal,
                and B. Schiele. "Recognizing Fine-Grained and Composite Activities Us-
                ing Hand-Centric Features and Script Data". In: *International Journal of
                Computer Vision (IJCV)* 119.3 (2016), pp. 346–373.

[Ros+08]   D. A. Ross, J. Lim, R.-S. Lin, and M.-H. Yang. "Incremental Learning for
                Robust Visual Tracking". In: *International Journal of Computer Vision (IJCV)*
                77.1 (2008), pp. 125–141.

[SAS07]   P. Scovanner, S. Ali, and M. Shah. "A 3-dimensional Sift Descriptor and
                Its Application to Action Recognition". In: *Multimedia, ACM International
                Conference on*. 2007, pp. 357–360.

[SCN08]   A. Saxena, S. H. Chung, and A. Y. Ng. "3-D Depth Reconstruction from a
                Single Still Image". In: *International Journal of Computer Vision (IJCV)* 76.1
                (2008), pp. 53–69.

[Sha+15]   J. Shao, K. Kang, C. C. Loy, and X. Wang. "Deeply learned attributes for
                crowded scene understanding". In: *Computer Vision and Pattern Recognition
                (CVPR), IEEE Conference on*. 2015, pp. 4657–4666.

[SKG16]   K. Shirahama, L. Köping, and M. Grzegorzek. "Codebook Approach for
                Sensor-based Human Activity Recognition". In: *Pervasive and Ubiquitous
                Computing: Adjunct, ACM International Joint Conference on*. 2016, pp. 197–
                200.

[SLW14]   J. Shao, C. C. Loy, and X. Wang. "Scene-Independent Group Profiling in
                Crowd". In: *Computer Vision and Pattern Recognition (CVPR), IEEE Confer-
                ence on*. 2014, pp. 2227–2234.

[SM14]   S. Song and M.Chandraker. "Robust Scale Estimation in Real-Time
                Monocular SFM for Autonomous Driving". In: *Computer Vision and Pattern
                Recognition (CVPR), IEEE Conference on*. 2014, pp. 1566–1573.

[SMO05]   P. Saisan, S. Medasani, and Y. Owechko. "Multi-View Classifier Swarms for Pedestrian Detection and Tracking". In: *Computer Vision and Pattern Recognition (CVPR), IEEE Conference on - Workshops*. 2005, pp. 18–18.

[SMS12]   B. Solmaz, B. E. Moore, and Mubarak Shah. "Identifying Behaviors in Crowd Scenes Using Stability Analysis for Dynamical Systems". In: *Pattern Analysis and Machine Intelligence (TPAMI), IEEE Transactions on* 34.10 (2012), pp. 2064–2070.

[SSN09]   A. Saxena, M. Sun, and A. Y. Ng. "Make3D: Learning 3D Scene Structure from a Single Still Image". In: *Pattern Analysis and Machine Intelligence (TPAMI), IEEE Transactions on* 31.5 (2009), pp. 824–840.

[SSP14]   T. Sattler, C. Sweeney, and M. Pollefeys. "On Sampling Focal Length Values to Solve the Absolute Pose Problem". In: *Computer Vision (ECCV), European Conference on*. 2014, pp. 828–843.

[STW07]   C. Shan, T. Tan, and Y. Wei. "Real-time hand tracking using a mean shift embedded particle filter". In: *Pattern Recognition* 40.7 (2007), pp. 1958–1970.

[SX13]   S. Song and J. Xiao. "Tracking Revisited Using RGBD Camera: Unified Benchmark and Baselines". In: *Computer Vision (ICCV), IEEE International Conference on*. 2013, pp. 233–240.

[SZ14]   K. Simonyan and A. Zisserman. "Very Deep Convolutional Networks for Large-Scale Image Recognition". In: *CoRR* abs/1409.1556 (2014).

[TK91]   C. Tomasi and T. Kanade. *Detection and Tracking of Point Features*. Tech. rep. International Journal of Computer Vision (IJCV), 1991.

[TS05]   P. Tissainayagam and D. Suter. "Object tracking in image sequences using point features". In: *Pattern Recognition* 38.1 (2005), pp. 105–113.

[Uij+13]   J. R. R. Uijlings, K. E. A. van de Sande, T. Gevers, and A. W. M. Smeulders. "Selective Search for Object Recognition". In: *International Journal of Computer Vision (IJCV)* 104.2 (2013), pp. 154–171.

[Ved+09]   A. Vedaldi, V. Gulshan, M. Varma, and A. Zisserman. "Multiple kernels for object detection". In: *Computer Vision (ICCV), IEEE International Conference on*. 2009, pp. 606–613.

[VF08]   A. Vedaldi and B. Fulkerson. *VLFeat: An Open and Portable Library of Computer Vision Algorithms*. http://www.vlfeat.org/. 2008.

[VJ04]   P. Viola and M. J. Jones. "Robust Real-Time Face Detection". In: *International Journal of Computer Vision (IJCV)* 57.2 (2004), pp. 137–154.

[Wan+11]   H. Wang, A. Kläser, C. Schmid, and C. L. Liu. "Action recognition by dense trajectories". In: *Computer Vision and Pattern Recognition (CVPR), IEEE Conference on*. 2011, pp. 3169–3176.

[Wan+14]   S. Wang, Z. Ma, Y. Yang, X. Li, C. Pang, and A. G. Hauptmann. "Semi-Supervised Multiple Feature Analysis for Action Recognition". In: *Multimedia, IEEE Transactions on* 16.2 (2014), pp. 289–298.

[Web]   Webster. *"human activity"*. http://www.webster-dictionary.org. On-line; accessed 09 March 2017.

[Whe+15]   T. Whelan, M. Kaess, H. Johannsson, M. Fallon, J. J. Leonard, and J. Mcdon-ald. "Real-time Large-scale Dense RGB-D SLAM with Volumetric Fusion". In: *The International Journal of Robotics Research* 34.4-5 (2015), pp. 598–626.

[WMG09]   X. Wang, X. Ma, and W. E. L. Grimson. "Unsupervised Activity Perception in Crowded and Complicated Scenes Using Hierarchical Bayesian Mod-els". In: *Pattern Analysis and Machine Intelligence (TPAMI), IEEE Transactions on* 31.3 (2009), pp. 539–555.

[Woj+11]   C. Wojek, S. Walk, S. Roth, and B. Schiele. "Monocular 3D Scene Un-derstanding with Explicit Occlusion Reasoning". In: *Computer Vision and Pattern Recognition (CVPR), IEEE Conference on*. 2011, pp. 1993–2000.

[Woj+13]   C. Wojek, S. Walk, S. Roth, K. Schindler, and B. Schiele. "Monocular Vi-sual Scene Understanding: Understanding Multi-Object Traffic Scenes". In: *Pattern Analysis and Machine Intelligence (TPAMI), IEEE Transactions on* 35.4 (2013), pp. 882–897.

[Wor+15]   S. Workman, C. Greenwell, M. Zhai, R. Baltenberger, and N. Jacobs. "DEEPFOCAL: A method for direct focal length estimation". In: *Image Processing (ICIP), IEEE International Conference on*. 2015, pp. 1369–1373.

[WOS11]   S. Wu, O. Oreifej, and M. Shah. "Action recognition in videos acquired by a moving camera using motion decomposition of Lagrangian particle trajectories". In: *Computer Vision (ICCV), IEEE International Conference on*. 2011, pp. 1419–1426.

[WS13]   H. Wang and C. Schmid. "Action Recognition with Improved Trajecto-ries". In: *Computer Vision (ICCV), IEEE International Conference on*. 2013, pp. 3551–3558.

[WZL16]   Y. Wang, Q. Zhang, and B. Li. "Efficient unsupervised abnormal crowd activity detection based on a spatiotemporal saliency detector". In: *Appli-cations of Computer Vision (WACV), IEEE Winter Conference on*. 2016, pp. 1–9.

[W*et al.*14] C. Wolf *et al.* "Evaluation of Video Activity Localizations Integrating Qual-ity and Quantity Measurements". In: *Computer Vision and Image Under-standing* 127 (2014), pp. 14–30.

[XG05]   T. Xiang and S. Gong. "Video behaviour profiling and abnormality detec-tion without manual labelling". In: *Computer Vision (CVPR), IEEE Interna-tional Conference on*. Vol. 2. 2005, pp. 1238–1245.

[XG08]   T. Xiang and S. Gong. "Incremental and adaptive abnormal behaviour de-tection". In: *Computer Vision and Image Understanding* 111.1 (2008), pp. 59–73.

[Xia+14]   Y. Xiang, C. Song, R. Mottaghi, and S. Savarese. "Monocular Multiview Object Tracking with 3D Aspect Parts". In: *Computer Vision (ECCV), Euro-pean Conference on*. 2014, pp. 220–235.

[XLS04]   A. Yilmaz Xin, X. Li, and M. Shah. "Object Contour Tracking Using Level Sets". In: *Computer Vision (ACCV), Asian Conference on*. 2004, pp. 1–1.

[Yi+14]   S. Yi, X. Wang, C. Lu, and J. Jia. "L0 Regularized Stationary Time Estimation for Crowd Group Analysis". In: *Computer Vision and Pattern Recognition (CVPR), IEEE Conference on*. 2014, pp. 2219–2226.

[YLW15a]   S. Yi, H. Li, and X. Wang. "Pedestrian Travel Time Estimation in Crowded Scenes". In: *Computer Vision (ICCV), IEEE International Conference on*. 2015, pp. 3137–3145.

[YLW15b]   S. Yi, H. Li, and X. Wang. "Understanding pedestrian behaviors from stationary crowd groups". In: *Computer Vision and Pattern Recognition (CVPR), IEEE Conference on*. 2015, pp. 3488–3496.

[YT14]   X. Yang and Y. Tian. "Super Normal Vector for Activity Recognition Using Depth Sequences". In: *Computer Vision and Pattern Recognition (CVPR), IEEE Conference on*. 2014, pp. 804–811.

[Zha+15]   S. Zhang, X. Yu, Y. Sui, S. Zhao, and L. Zhang. "Object Tracking With Multi-View Support Vector Machines". In: *Multimedia, IEEE Transactions on* 17.3 (2015), pp. 265–278.

[Zhe15]   Y. Zheng. "Trajectory Data Mining: An Overview". In: *Intelligent Systems and Technology (TIST), ACM Transactions on* 6.3 (2015), pp. 1–41.

[ZK15]   Q.-Y. Zhou and V. Koltun. "Depth camera tracking with contour cues". In: *Computer Vision and Pattern Recognition (CVPR), IEEE Conference on*. 2015, pp. 632–638.

[ZWT12]   B. Zhou, X. Wang, and X. Tang. "Understanding collective crowd behaviors: Learning a Mixture model of Dynamic pedestrian-Agents". In: *Computer Vision and Pattern Recognition (CVPR), IEEE Conference on*. 2012, pp. 2871–2878.

Own Publications

[Bou+15a]   Zeyd Boukhers, Kimiaki Shirahama, Frédéric Li, and Marcin Grzegorzek. "Extracting 3D Trajectories of Objects from 2D Videos Using Particle Filter". In: *Multimedia Retrieval(ICMR), ACM International Conference on*. 2015, pp. 83–90.

[Bou+15b]   Zeyd Boukhers, Kimiaki Shirahama, Frédéric Li, and Marcin Grzegorzek. "Object detection and depth estimation for 3D trajectory extraction". In: *Content-Based Multimedia Indexing (CBMI), International Workshop on*. 2015, pp. 1–6.

[Bou+16a]   Zeyd Boukhers, Yicong Wang, Kimiaki Shirahama, Kuniaki Uehara, and Marcin Grzegorzek. "Convoy Detection in Crowded Surveillance Videos". In: *Human Behavior Understanding, International Workshop on, at ACM Multimedia*. 2016, pp. 137–147.

[Bou+16b]   Zeyd Boukhers, Tomasz Jarzyński, Florian Schmidt, Oliver Tiebe, and Marcin Grzegorzek. "Shape-Based Eye Blinking Detection and Analysis". In: *Computer Recognition Systems (CORES), International Conference on*. 2016, pp. 327–335.

[BSG17a]   Zeyd Boukhers, Kimiaki Shirahama, and Marcin Grzegorzek. "Example-based 3D Trajectory Extraction of Objects from 2D Videos". In: *Circuits and Systems for Videos Technology (TCSVT), IEEE Transaction on* PP.99 (2017), pp. 1–1.

[BSG17b]   Zeyd Boukhers, Kimiaki Shirahama, and Marcin Grzegorzek. "Less Restrictive Camera Odometry from Monocular Camera". In: *Multimedia Tools and Applications* PP.99 (2017), pp. 1–1.

[Kha+16]   Muhammad Hassan Khan, Jullien Helsper, Zeyd Boukhers, and Marcin Grzegorzek. "Automatic recognition of movement patterns in the vojta-therapy using RGB-D data". In: *Image Processing (ICIP), IEEE International Conference on*. 2016, pp. 1235–1239.

[Zou+16]   Yan Ling Zou, Chen Li, Zeyd Boukhers, Kimiaki Shirahama, Tao Jiang, and Marcin Grzegorzek. "Environmental Microbiological Content-Based Image Retrieval System Using Internal Structure Histogram". In: *Computer Recognition Systems (CORES), International Conference on*. 2016, pp. 543–552.

Curriculum Vitae

Personal Data

Last Name, First Name	Boukhers, Zeyd
Nationality	Algerian
Date, Place of Birth	25th April 1987, Oran

Education

October 2013 - September 2017	*PhD Candidate* Research Group for Pattern Recognition University of Siegen, Siegen, Germany
September 2008 - July 2011	*Student of Pattern Recognition and Artificial Intelligence (Master)* University of Science and Technology of Oran, Oran, Algeria
September 2005 - July 2008	*Student of Computer Science (Bachelor)* University of Science and Technology of Oran, Oran, Algeria
September 2001 - June 2005	*High School Student in Nature and Life Science* High School Mustapha Haddam, Oran, Algeria
September 1998 - June 2001	*Middle School Student* Middle School Fellaoucene, Oran, Algeria
September 1992 - June 1998	*Primary School Student* Primary School Fellaoucene I, II, Oran, Algeria

Professional Experience & Academic Activities

January 2016 - March 2016

Visiting Researcher
Kobe University,
Kobe, Japan

September 2010 - March 2013

Lecturer of Computer Science
University of Oran,
Oran, Algeria

September 2010 - March 2013

Developing Manager
IT& B,
Oran, Algeria

September 2009 - July 2010

Lecturer of Computer Science
Microway School,
Oran, Algeria

In der Reihe *Studien zur Mustererkennung,*
herausgegeben von
Prof. Dr. Ing Heinricht Niemann und Herrn Prof. Dr. Ing. Elmar Nöth
sind bisher erschienen:

1	Jürgen Haas	Probabilistic Methods in Linguistic Analysis
		ISBN 978-3-89722-565-7, 2000, 260 S. 40.50 €
2	Manuela Boros	Partielles robustes Parsing spontansprachlicher Dialoge am Beispiel von Zugauskunftdialogen
		ISBN 978-3-89722-600-5, 2001, 264 S. 40.50 €
3	Stefan Harbeck	Automatische Verfahren zur Sprachdetektion, Landessprachenerkennung und Themendetektion
		ISBN 978-3-89722-766-8, 2001, 260 S. 40.50 €
4	Julia Fischer	Ein echtzeitfähiges Dialogsystem mit iterativer Ergebnisoptimierung
		ISBN 978-3-89722-867-2, 2002, 222 S. 40.50 €
5	Ulrike Ahlrichs	Wissensbasierte Szenenexploration auf der Basis erlernter Analysestrategien
		ISBN 978-3-89722-904-4, 2002, 165 S. 40.50 €
6	Florian Gallwitz	Integrated Stochastic Models for Spontaneous Speech Recognition
		ISBN 978-3-89722-907-5, 2002, 196 S. 40.50 €
7	Uwe Ohler	Computational Promoter Recognition in Eukaryotic Genomic DNA
		ISBN 978-3-89722-988-4, 2002, 206 S. 40.50 €
8	Richard Huber	Prosodisch-linguistische Klassifikation von Emotion
		ISBN 978-3-89722-984-6, 2002, 293 S. 40.50 €

9   Volker Warnke   Integrierte Segmentierung und Klassifikation von Äußerungen und Dialogakten mit heterogenen Wissensquellen

ISBN 978-3-8325-0254-6, 2003, 182 S.   40.50 €

10 Michael Reinhold   Robuste, probabilistische, erscheinungsbasierte Objekterkennung

ISBN 978-3-8325-0476-2, 2004, 283 S.   40.50 €

11 Matthias Zobel   Optimale Brennweitenwahl für die multiokulare Objektverfolgung

ISBN 978-3-8325-0496-0, 2004, 292 S.   40.50 €

12 Bernd Ludwig   Ein konfigurierbares Dialogsystem für Mensch-Maschine-Interaktion in gesprochener Sprache

ISBN 978-3-8325-0497-7, 2004, 230 S.   40.50 €

13 Rainer Deventer   Modeling and Control of Static and Dynamic Systems with Bayesian Networks

ISBN 978-3-8325-0521-9, 2004, 195 S.   40.50 €

14 Jan Buckow   Multilingual Prosody in Automatic Speech Understanding

ISBN 978-3-8325-0581-3, 2004, 164 S.   40.50 €

15 Klaus Donath   Automatische Segmentierung und Analyse von Blutgefäßen

ISBN 978-3-8325-0642-1, 2004, 210 S.   40.50 €

16 Axel Walthelm   Sensorbasierte Lokalisations-Algorithmen für mobile Service-Roboter

ISBN 978-3-8325-0691-9, 2004, 200 S.   40.50 €

17 Ricarda Dormeyer   Syntaxanalyse auf der Basis der Dependenzgrammatik

ISBN 978-3-8325-0723-7, 2004, 200 S.   40.50 €

18 Michael Levit   Spoken Language Understanding without Transcriptions in a Call Center Scenario

ISBN 978-3-8325-0930-9, 2005, 249 S.   40.50 €

Alle erschienenen Bücher können unter der angegebenen ISBN im Buchhandel oder di-
rekt beim Logos Verlag Berlin (www.logos-verlag.de, Fax: 030 - 42 85 10 92) bestellt werden.